31
DAYS
OF
PRAYER
FOR MY
Husband

BroadStreet
PUBLISHING

BroadStreet Publishing Group, LLC
Savage, Minnesota, USA
BroadStreetPublishing.com

31 DAYS OF PRAYER FOR MY *Husband*

Copyright © 2018 Great Commandment Network

9781424565689 faux leather
9781424555963 softcover
9781424555970 e-book

Design and typesetting by Garborg Design Works, Inc. | garborgdesign.com
Revised and edited by Michelle Winger | literallyprecise.com

Printed in China

22 23 24 25 5 4 3 2 1

CONTENTS

A SPIRIT-EMPOWERED DISCIPLE
LOVES PEOPLE

A SPIRIT-EMPOWERED DISCIPLE
LIVES HIS MISSION

INTRODUCTION

Marriage is one of the most exciting relationships God has created; yet all marriages could use more of God, more of His Word, and more Christlike attitudes that put each other first. That's why we've written *31 Days of Prayer for My Husband*.

We've served hundreds of thousands of couples with training events and resources, and it's confirmed: every couple wants a strong, intimate, thriving marriage! Too often though, in their search for closeness, many couples find themselves asking the wrong question.

Could it be that an enriched, deepened marriage full of joy, intimacy, and fulfillment is realized not by focusing on and answering the question "How do I get the most out of my marriage" but by answering the question "How does God get what He wants out of my marriage?" Through this resource, we give you a daily opportunity to hear God's perspective about your husband and your marriage. Inviting the Creator of marriage *into* a marriage is always a good idea!

Finally, we've also designed *31 Days of Prayer for My Husband* for your enrichment, encouragement, and growth. As you spend time with Jesus, in His Word, your life will forever be changed.

May God richly bless your time with Jesus and your relationship with your husband.

Terri Snead
Executive Editor, Great Commandment Network

The Great Commandment Network is an international collaborative network of strategic kingdom leaders from the faith community, marketplace, education, and caregiving fields who prioritize the powerful simplicity of the words of Jesus to love God, love others, and see people become His followers (Matthew 22:37–40; 28:19–20).

Day 1

WHY I SHOULD PRAY
FOR MY HUSBAND

Why is it important to dedicate the time or make it a priority to pray for your husband? Setting aside thirty-one days to pray for him makes sense for many reasons. Here are just a few:

- **As you pray** for your husband, you're joining Jesus as He prays on his behalf.

Hebrews says, "He lives forever to intercede with God on [our] behalf" (Hebrews 7:25). In the book of Romans, Paul writes, "he is sitting in the place of honor at God's right hand, pleading for us" (8:34). Don't you imagine the Savior's prayer list includes your husband? When you pray, you have the privilege of joining Jesus in prayer for him.

- **As you pray** for your husband, you're joining Jesus in His celebrations.

In Christ's last moments on earth, He revealed His loving desire for His followers: "that my joy may be in you, and that your joy may be made full" (John 15:11 NASB). Jesus finds joy in your husband and in your marriage. Since marriage is a special representation of Christ's love for the church, Jesus feels a special joy when He sees marriages thriving. He loves when your relationship is a testimony to a hurting world. When you pray, you have the privilege of joining Jesus in a celebration of the beauty of marriage. (See Proverbs 18:22; James 1:17.)

- **As you pray** for your husband, you're joining Jesus in His concern.

Jesus feels compassion for the struggles in your marriage and any challenges your husband might be facing. His heart is moved with compassion when He sees your groom hurting, disappointed, discouraged, or alone. So join Jesus in praying, lifting up concerns and asking the Lord to give you a deeper understanding of your husband. Praying for him allows the Holy Spirit to help you see what He sees, so you can love him the way that Jesus loves. (See 2 Corinthians 1:2–4.)

- **As you pray** for your husband, you strengthen your own walk with Jesus.

Spending time with your Savior deepens your closeness with Him. As you pray, the Spirit will minister to your heart, to your needs, and to your concerns. So, pray for your husband! Pray often. Pray consistently. Pray boldly. And pray faithfully. (See Romans 8:26–27.)

Take the next few moments and join Jesus in prayer.

* Jesus, when I imagine that I can join you in prayer, my heart feels grateful because _____.

* I want to join you in prayer for my husband. First, I'm grateful *for* my husband because _____.

* I lift up my husband to you and pray specifically that you would _____.

Day 2

HOW TO PRAY
FOR MY HUSBAND

A world in which the prince of darkness seeks to steal, kill, and destroy, needs Christ-followers who walk in the light (John 10:10; 12:35 NASB). For the next thirty-one days, be encouraged to take a journey of walking in the light. During your times of prayer, you will walk in the light of God's Son, God's Word, and God's people (John 8:12; Matthew 5:14; Psalm 119:105). As you take the journey, you will spend moments in personal prayer and in prayer for your husband. You'll pray for him to

- encounter Jesus in fresh, new ways,
- live out the Bible frequently, and
- interact with people in supportive, practical ways.

Have a first encounter with Jesus. As you read these words from the Savior, imagine that He is speaking directly to you. Listen for His compassionate, strong voice. He's thrilled to share these moments just with you.

PRAY AND LISTEN TO JESUS

The darkness of this world is all around you, and I don't want you to be overtaken. So I have a plan. I have a plan for your protection, guidance, and strength. If you'll spend time with me, my Word, and my people, darkness won't have a chance. As you encounter me, I will protect you because I'm the Light of the World. Let my Word guide you and light your way. Let my people encourage you and give you strength. Walking in the light is the best place to be because that means we're walking together. (See John 8:12; Matthew 5:14; Psalm 119:105.)

* Jesus, when I look at the darkness of this world, I feel especially concerned about _____.

* Lord, I am grateful for your protection, guidance, and strength, particularly because _____.

* Jesus, I pray that my husband would spend more quality time with you, your Word, and your people, so darkness doesn't have a chance in our home or in our marriage.

* I pray you would protect my husband from _____.

* I pray you would guide my husband in _____.

* I pray you would strengthen my husband in _____.

As you continue this journey of prayer, remember the goal. Your times of prayer can't be focused on changing your husband. These moments with Jesus and His Word are designed to first develop Christlikeness in you. The destination of your journey is a person, and His name is Jesus. As you spend time focused on getting to know Christ and experiencing more of His love, and as you spend time living out His Word, not just reading or hearing it, you'll become like Him. This journey will change something—and hopefully it's you!

Finally, as you take this journey of prayer, it will also be important to remember this goal: your husband doesn't need more things to do or more assessments of his behavior. He rarely needs to hear more information or rational advice. He will change as he encounters Jesus, His Word, and His people.

You may be thinking, *My husband needs to change in some areas. Our marriage needs to be stronger in specific ways. If I can't give advice or information or assessment, what can I do?*

Pray. Have your own encounters with Jesus and see what changes He might want to make in you.

Live. Consistently live out God's Word and do the Bible in your home and marriage. Watch His Word make a difference.

Act. Use the ideas from this resource and take action steps. Take initiative to love your husband in practical, relevant ways.

Pray, live, and act. Then watch the power of God's Son, His Word, and His people make a difference in your husband and in your marriage.

Day 3

WHAT TO PRAY
FOR MY HUSBAND

This book is designed to foster a Spirit-empowered faith—a faith that is demonstrable, observable, and only possible with the empowerment of the Holy Spirit. A framework for this kind of spiritual growth has been drawn from a cluster analysis of several Greek and Hebrew words that declare that Christ's followers are to be equipped for works of ministry or service. (See Ephesians 4:12.) Therefore, in this book you'll find specific sections that are designed around four themes. (See Appendix 3.) A Spirit-empowered disciple:

- **Loves the Lord** by talking to and listening to God for daily decisions and direction for life (Luke 10:38–42). You will find seven days of prayer marked L-2.
- **Lives the Word** by demonstrating a love for God's Word and living it out every day (2 Corinthians 3:2). You will find seven days of prayer marked W-2.
- **Loves People** by discerning relational needs of others and sharing God's love in meaningful ways (Ephesians 4:29). You will find seven days of prayer marked P-3.

- **Lives His Mission** by actively sharing their lives with others and telling them about the Jesus who lives inside of them (1 Thessalonians 2:8). You will find seven days of prayer marked M-1.

The world needs couples living as Spirit-empowered disciples who are making disciples who, in turn, make more disciples. Thus, this book rightly focuses on the powerful simplicity of

- loving God as your first priority,
- living His Word because there's power and possibility in experiencing Scripture,
- loving people by developing a lifestyle of giving first to your husband and then to others around you, and
- living His mission, which means building a lasting legacy.

After three days of prayer focused on why, how, and what to pray for your husband, you will turn your attention to specific prayer themes. Before you focus on these thematic prayers, live out God's Word. God says that if you ask anything according to His will, He hears you and grants your request (1 John 5:14–15). You know it's His will for you to love your husband well, so you can count on Him to grant this request. Spend the next few moments in prayer. Make your request to God and look for how He gives to you. "If you ask the Father for anything in my name, he will give it to you" (John 16:23 NASB).

LIVE: DO THE BIBLE

God, I know it's your will for me to love my husband well, so I'm asking you to give me whatever I need to do that. If I need to change, show me. If I need to see things differently, I'm ready. I'm asking these things in your name, knowing that you will answer my prayer and give me what I ask. In Jesus' name. Amen.

Notes

A SPIRIT-EMPOWERED DISCIPLE

Loves the Lord

Day 4

PRAYING TOGETHER

Talk to and listen to God for your daily decisions and direction for life, especially in regard to your spiritual closeness.

STORIES FROM A WIFE'S HEART

My parents had an awful marriage. My father was weak and distant, and my mother was too controlling. I mistakenly felt it was my calling to keep my own marriage from suffering the same fate. At first, my comments to my husband were helpful, but slowly he became withdrawn.

Through the help of our mentors, we learned that we were locked into a cycle of hurting one another in one of the most painful ways possible: in ways that each of us had been hurt before. When I criticized my husband, it was magnified by the pain of criticism he had endured as a child. As my husband withdrew from me, it touched the pain of my dad's distance from me in my growing-up years.

After participating in a couples' intensive retreat, my husband and I came to see each other's pain, and we were able to offer each other words of compassion. We learned to pray together and seek the Lord for His comfort. We experienced the joy of bringing our burdens to God and then trusting Him to make changes in our marriage.

PRAY: LISTEN TO JESUS

I long to have quiet moments of conversation with you and your husband. I love when you are still and free of distractions because those are the times when you can truly feel my love. I especially enjoy seeing you pray together as a couple. When the three of us come together in prayer, miraculous things can happen. Remember, I am the God of love. So it's in these quiet moments of time with me that I can be your unlimited source of sacrificial love. (See Psalm 46:10; 1 John 4:8.)

* Jesus, I ask that you quiet my mind and spirit. Help me to focus on you. In my relationship with my husband, I am depending upon you to _____. Since you are the God of love, I am counting on you to _____.

* Lord, I pray for my husband. Would you draw him closer to you? Since you are the God of love, I ask that you empower him to _____.

LIVE: DO THE BIBLE

Are any of you suffering hardships? You should pray.

—James 5:13

* God, I come to you now about the hardships I am enduring. I need to know that you care about them. Please reassure

me of your love. I need you to intervene in this situation, and empower me with your love because _____.

* God, in the same way, I pray for my husband. He needs to know that you care. Please reassure him of your love. He needs you to intervene in this situation and empower him with your love because _____.

TAKE ACTION

• Invite your husband to talk with you about the spiritual goals you both have (e.g., more times of prayer together, Bible study, devotionals, church attendance, etc.). Implement one of these ideas this week.

• Invite your husband to lead out in prayer. Spend several minutes discussing the most pressing needs and hardships of your life together and then pray.

CLAIM HIS PROMISES

Come near to God and he will come near to you.

—JAMES 4:8 NIV

Love the Lord L-2:
A Spirit-empowered disciple listens to and hears God for daily decisions and direction for life.

Day 5

CELEBRATE YOUR DIFFERENCES

Talk to and listen to God for your daily decisions and direction for life, especially as you navigate the ways in which you are different.

STORIES FROM A WIFE'S HEART

Over the years, my husband and I have wasted a lot of time and words arguing about whose thoughts and ideas are better. We've had arguments over every imaginable marriage issue, including such things as, "There's no gas in the car," "The dishes don't go in the dishwasher that way," and "Why didn't you call and let me know they were coming over?" Our list of marital issues can sometimes seem endless, but even though we've been slow learners, we've found a better way.

We begin with the principle that neither of us has thoughts, ideas, and plans that are best. They may be good, but they are not God's thoughts and therefore can't be perfect. The bottom line is, God's thoughts, ideas, and plans are second to none. The famed missionary George Mueller prayed this way: "Father, I have my thoughts about this issue, but I want your thoughts. I don't want to have my own will about the matter—I want your will." In our marriage, we strive to have God's thoughts about any issue, not just our own. We pray for His will about a matter, because His ways are perfect and always for our good.

As we prayerfully approach the Lord in this way, He brings us together and causes His ways to prevail. As we've learned to approach the disagreements of our marriage in this way, we've not only enjoyed more harmony, but we've also come to appreciate one another's perspectives. I've come to greatly appreciate my husband's vision, passion, boldness, and get-it-done attitude. I would not have come to fully appreciate these strengths in him had we not spent time together seeking God's thoughts, ideas, and plans.

PRAY: LISTEN TO JESUS

Humble yourself, and I will lift you up. I love it when you acknowledge your dependence on me. I can't wait to come to your aid. I am ready to teach you my ways and lead you in how to celebrate the differences between you and your husband. Your humility is what moves me to action. I keep my distance from the proud. So talk freely about how you need me and are depending on me. (See James 4:10; Psalm 25:9; 69:32; 138:6; Isaiah 55:8; 1 Peter 3:7.)

* Jesus, please show me your ways and your thoughts. Especially when I'm tempted to think that my ways are best, reveal your perspective. I need to specifically hear you concerning _____.

* Lord, I pray for my husband and our marriage. We are depending on you to help us navigate our differences. We especially need your help concerning _____.

LIVE: DO THE BIBLE

We are God's masterpiece. He has created us anew in Christ Jesus, so we can do the good things he planned for us long ago.

—EPHESIANS 2:10

* God, I want to see my husband as your masterpiece. Show me the traits about him that make you particularly proud. Show me, Lord. I am celebrating these unique characteristics about my husband: _____.

* God, in the same way, I pray that my husband would see me as a unique creation of yours. Bring unity in our relationship particularly in how we _____.

* Lord, you have planned good things for each of us to do. Increase our unity and help us celebrate our differences, so we might point more and more people to you.

TAKE ACTION

• If you have a question or concern about your husband's decisions, lovingly discuss it in private.

• Write down the improvements or changes that you could make that would help your marriage communication especially regarding the ways you are different.

- Look for an opportunity to defer to your husband. Say something like, "We're really different in this area, and yet I want to give to you by _____."

CLAIM HIS PROMISES

You faithfully answer our prayers with awesome deeds, O God our savior.

—PSALM 65:5

Love the Lord L-2:
A Spirit-empowered disciple listens to and hears God for daily decisions and direction for life.

Day 6

GOALS AND PLANS

Talk to and listen to God for your daily decisions and direction for life especially in regard to goals for your future.

STORIES FROM A WIFE'S HEART

Developing and maintaining an intimate marriage requires a consistent investment of time and emotional energy. Our marriage relationship dramatically improved when we began what we called our weekly "marriage staff meetings." We didn't leave the meetings to chance, instead making this time together a priority. We avoided distractions and interruptions and chose a place that was the most quiet and protected.

Consistency was important, but the emotional benefit of prioritizing each other encouraged our closeness. As I heard my husband turn down engagements with friends so that we could keep our marriage staff meetings, my heart was incredibly blessed. When he saw that I didn't even take my cell phone into our staff meetings, he felt loved and reassured that I had concern for him and for our relationship.

You might be thinking, *What in the world would we talk about?* Here are some topics you might want to try:

- Coordinate calendars: discuss kids' schedules, church attendance, and community events.
- Family goals: discuss financial savings, vacation ideas, and landscaping plans.
- Parenting plans: discuss discipline issues and spiritual training.
- Affirm one another: share appreciation and approval.

PRAY: LISTEN TO JESUS

I love to see the plans you make, especially as you include me. It brings me joy to give you the desires of your heart and make your plans succeed. It's a part of my divine nature to bring good things to your life. So seek me out, include me in your plans because I long to meet your needs.

Harmony is precious to me, beloved. I love seeing my people make decisions in unity. If you're having trouble, remember that my Holy Spirit is interceding on your behalf. He's praying for you and your husband. His prayers are meant to help you live according to my will. (See Matthew 6:33; Psalm 20:4, 133:2; Romans 8:27.)

* Jesus, I know you have good things planned for us, and I'm grateful. You've been faithful to give us _____. Grant us wisdom now as we make plans to _____.

* Lord, I pray that my husband and I would come together in harmony around these goals: _____. Thank you that your Spirit is interceding for us about _____.

LIVE: DO THE BIBLE

I will seek the one I love.

—SONG OF SOLOMON 3:2

* God, I want to seek your counsel about this goal: _____. Help me to know the best way and best time to seek my husband's input about our plans for _____.

* God, in the same way, I pray that my husband would hear from you about _____. Show us the plans you have for us. We want to hear what you have to say about _____. Bring us to unity, Lord. We want to please you with the harmony of our marriage.

TAKE ACTION

* Ask your husband to discuss plans for a special date night. Meet your goal for increased closeness.

* Ask your husband's input about the specific character traits that need to be emphasized as you train each of your children. Discuss plans for parenting in these ways.

* Write down your response to this statement: "If all my dreams for the future could come true, here's what our life, marriage, and family would look like: _____." Ask your husband to do the same, and then talk through both responses.

CLAIM HIS PROMISES

For I know the plans I have for you, says the Lord. They are plans for good and not for evil, to give you a future and a hope.

—JEREMIAH 29:11 TLB

Love the Lord L-2:
A Spirit-empowered disciple listens to and hears God for daily decisions and direction for life.

Day 7

ATTITUDE
OF GRATITUDE

Talk to and listen to God for your daily decisions and direction for life.
Cultivate a spirit of gratitude and thanksgiving.

STORIES FROM A WIFE'S HEART

Wonder and awe must have been at least part of what Mary felt when she made her joyful declaration to God, "My soul magnifies the Lord" (Luke 1:46 ESV). Mary's exaltation and gratitude were not about possessions or position, but about relationship. As the most blessed of all women, Mary's blessing came through a divinely provided relationship. Her exaltation and worship were responses to gifts from the Father.

In a similar way, we who are married have been divinely blessed with the spouse God has uniquely provided. The apostle James reminds us that every good and perfect gift comes down from the Father above (James 1:17). The same God who blessed Mary with His announcement of Christ has given me one of His most special gifts.

More and more frequently, I've recognized a sense of deep gratitude for my husband. He's a partner who has seen my rough side and still accepts me; a partner whose strengths lovingly balance my weaknesses; and a partner who thinks of me, gives to me, and cares about me. He's the gift God has given me. Because of this, my soul magnifies the Lord.

PRAY: LISTEN TO JESUS

In case you're unsure of how to connect with me, I've given you a hint. Thank me. I've given you everything you enjoy— every breath you breathe and every relationship you call dear. It's my absolute joy to give, yet it hurts my heart when the ones I love forget to say thank you. I feel loved and honored when I hear your words of gratitude. My followers who have learned to acclaim me walk in my presence and find great blessing. Your gratitude keeps us close. (See Psalm 50:23, 69:30, 89:15; 1 Thessalonians 5:18.)

* Jesus, I don't ever want you to feel disappointed because I forget to say thank you. When I imagine how much you have given to me and my family, and how you might experience hurt because of my lack of gratitude, I feel _____.

* Lord, I don't want to forget to say thank you for my husband. He is a gift from you. Remind me of all the ways he is a special blessing from you to me. Keep me from being critical. I'm grateful you found and provided him for me because _____.

LIVE: DO THE BIBLE

I will praise God's name with singing,
and I will honor him with thanksgiving.

—PSALM 69:30

* God, I want to bring you honor with my gratitude. Remind me of some of the special ways you have loved me recently. Today, I am particularly grateful for these ten things: _____.

* God, in the same way, I pray for my husband. Move his heart with gratefulness for how you have loved him well. I want him to enjoy the blessing of walking in your presence. I want him to receive the joy of special connection with you because _____.

TAKE ACTION

* Tell your husband some of the ways that he is a blessing to you. Share the top ten reasons he is God's gift.

* Brag on your husband and how you've been blessed by him. Share a post on social media or find some other public way to demonstrate your gratitude. Brag in front of your kids, family members, or friends: "I've recently been reminded of some of the great qualities in my husband. I'm grateful God gave him to me because _____."

CLAIM HIS PROMISES

"Giving thanks is a sacrifice that truly honors me.
If you keep to my path,
I will reveal to you the salvation of God."

—PSALM 50:23

Love the Lord L-2:
A Spirit-empowered disciple listens to and hears God for daily decisions and direction for life.

Day 8

A STUDENT OF MY HUSBAND

Talk to and listen to God for your daily decisions and direction for life, especially as you live out the kindness of the Lord.

STORIES FROM A WIFE'S HEART

In marriage, kindness means discerning the unique needs of a specific person. It involves taking the initiative to express care based on what you know of your spouse Kindness in marriage depends on you becoming a lifelong "student" of your husband—seeking to understand him, so you can best love him.

The apostle Peter referred to this when he encouraged husbands to "live with your wives in an understanding way" (1 Peter 3:7 NASB). Proverbs encourages a wife to "[look] well to the ways of her household" (31:27 NASB). This kind of understanding paves the way for lovingkindness in a marriage.

I can show my husband kindness like no one else because I know him so well. For example, I know the shirts he likes and how he needs to have a few minutes of down time after work. I know he likes to hang out with his buddies, but there are a few couples who he enjoys as well. I know he prefers to drive, but after a business trip he feels loved if I take the wheel. These demonstrations of kindness are possible because I've learned to be a student of my husband.

LISTEN TO JESUS

Remember, my beloved. I am wonderfully kind, patient, and tolerant of you. It was my kindness, in spite of your sin, that first drew you into a relationship with me. Now I'm giving you the opportunity to share some of that kindness with your husband. Pay it forward every day. Look for ways to demonstrate kindness. Be generous as I am generous. Take thought of him just as I think of you a thousand times a day. Finally, remember that sharing truth is important, but that it needs to be coupled with kindness. (See Romans 2:4; Proverbs 3:3; Ephesians 4:15; Psalm 139:17.)

* Jesus, you are so right. You have been patient, kind, and tolerant of me even though I _____. I am grateful for your kindness toward me because _____. I pray that you would empower me to demonstrate this same kindness in my marriage. I need your help to _____.

* Lord, I pray that my husband would have a fresh experience with your kindness as well. May he sense your patience and understanding and the generous way you love us both. I pray specifically that he would sense your kindness related to _____.

LIVE: DO THE BIBLE

Be kind to each other, tenderhearted, forgiving one another, just as God through Christ has forgiven you.

—EPHESIANS 4:32

* God, remind me often of my husband's preferences and uniquenesses. Show me the things I need to understand about him. Based on these special things, show me ways I can demonstrate your kindness. Show me how to be respectful and honoring of him. Show me any areas where I need to forgive, just like you've forgiven me. Speak to me, Lord. I'm listening for_____.

* Lord, I pray for my husband. Give him a fresh experience of your kindness and tenderness. I want him to soak in your forgiveness. Show him more and more of the ways he is loved by you so that _____.

TAKE ACTION

- Give your husband an unexpected hug, back rub, or foot massage. Initiate sex.

- Serve your husband his favorite meal.

- Compliment your husband on his appearance.

- Praise your husband for his accomplishment or achievement.

CLAIM HIS PROMISES

Those who are kind benefit themselves,
but the cruel bring ruin on themselves.

—Proverbs 11:17 NIV

Love the Lord L-2:
A Spirit-empowered disciple listens to and hears God for daily decisions and direction for life.

Day 9

HOPE INTO FAITH

Talk to and listen to God for your daily decisions and direction for life. Learn how to turn hope into faith.

STORIES FROM A WIFE'S HEART

During our first mentoring session with one couple, we identified common but painful dynamics in their relationship. Their expectations of one another were "killing us." The husband said, "She expects dinner out twice a week, so I give it to her whether or not we can afford it." The wife replied, "He expects sex twice a week, so I accommodate him whether or not I feel like it."

God has certainly created you with the capacity to bless your husband by meeting his needs, but your expectations are to be directed toward Him not your husband. God is the One who has promised to meet all your needs (Philippians 4:19). In His sovereignty, He may seek to involve your husband, but you are not to build your expectations around him.

This husband and wife were trying to take from one another. We told them that God's desire, in contrast, was for them to trust

Him with their needs. They would know they were demonstrating trust in God as they began to focus on giving. Their hopes would turn into faith as they trusted Him to meet their needs while focusing on giving to one another. Gratefully, they started trusting their needs to God and giving to each other. As a result, their marriage began to thrive.

PRAY: LISTEN TO JESUS

Trust me completely, then look for how I will provide. I am your security; you can count on my faithfulness. My faithfulness is as enduring as the heavens. Your demonstration of faith in me makes my heart sing. There are great blessings in store for the ones who put their faith in me: the faith-filled receive my protection, my favor, and a place of undeserved privilege. Place your faith in me and my Word and watch the things you hope for come into reality. (See Philippians 4:19; Proverbs 2:8, 3:26; Psalm 89:2; Matthew 8:10; Romans 5:2; Hebrews 11:1, 6.)

* Jesus, I want to please you, so I am trusting you in this area of my life: _____. I'm trusting you in this area of my marriage: _____. Please show me in your Word, how the things I hope for can be turned into demonstrations of faith in you (see Romans 15:4).

* Lord, I also pray that my husband would have a fresh sense of your faithfulness. I pray he would feel your blessing as he puts his trust in you. Empower him to put his faith in you regarding _____.

LIVE: DO THE BIBLE

Faith shows the reality of what we hope for; it is the evidence of things we cannot see.

—Hebrews 11:1

* God, as I consider my relationship with my husband, I am hoping for _____. Because I know that my faith pleases you, I am counting on you to _____.

* Lord, I ask that you would give my husband the same vision. I know he is hoping for _____ as it relates to our life together. Please reveal how he might demonstrate more faith in you, so he can please you.

TAKE ACTION

• Ask your husband what he is hoping for more of in your marriage and family. Seek the Lord's wisdom about how to make those changes.

• Memorize specific Bible promises that you are longing to see happen.

CLAIM HIS PROMISES

"If you have faith the size of a mustard seed, you will tell this mountain, 'Move from here to there,' and it will move. Nothing will be impossible for you."

—Matthew 17:20 hcsb

Love the Lord L-2:

A Spirit-empowered disciple listens to and hears God for daily decisions and direction for life.

Day 10

UNWRAPPING
YOUR GIFTS

Talk to and listen to God for your daily decisions and direction for life, and especially about your gifts.

STORIES FROM A WIFE'S HEART

Have you ever played the "Who's going to get up and take care of the baby?" game? Let me describe it for you. You and your spouse are dead tired from the daily rigors of life. The baby has been asleep for hours, and you have both nodded off. Suddenly, that little bundle of joy decides it is time to interact with you again. You lie there pretending you are sound asleep, hoping and praying your spouse will get up to feed and change the baby.

My husband and I have played that game hundreds of times. We've both mastered our personal techniques of pretending to be asleep. No matter who gets up in the middle of the night, my husband and I have concluded that this willingness to get up every time one of the babies cries has huge implications. It is our way of putting sacrificial love into practice.

That really is love, and it isn't easy. When you are tired, unappreciated, and have already gone the distance to take care of someone's needs, and then readily give one more time—that's love. Sacrificial love for my husband is easier when I remember Christ's sacrificial love for me and that my husband is a gift from Him.

PRAY: LISTEN TO JESUS

There's nothing stronger than a parent's love for his or her child. In fact, I see that love every time our Father looks at you. I also see the joy in your face when you take time to truly see your own children. Children are some of the Father's most precious gifts, so be sure to unwrap and admire them. Parenting is hard, so let me be your provider and guide. Just ask me for help, for I love to give it to you. (See Psalm 25:5, 127:3; Matthew 7:11.)

* Jesus, I want to demonstrate the kind of love you have for me to my children. Remind me often of the Father's love and then help me live that out in my family. Help me demonstrate love so that there is security and peace in my home. I especially need your help in this area: _____.

* Lord, I pray that you would often remind my husband of your love so he is free, empowered by your Spirit, and equipped with your wisdom to parent our kids in the ways they need it most. Our kids need _____, so please give my husband _____.

LIVE: DO THE BIBLE

Children are a gift from God; they are his reward.

—Psalm 127:3 TLB

* Jesus, please help me to unwrap the gifts you have given me. Slow me down so I can truly know them. What about my children do you want me to admire? What do you want me to see about their needs? Their futures? How can I come alongside my husband and parent well?

* Lord, I pray that you would equip my husband and me to slow down and unwrap each of our children as gifts from you. Give us divine insight into their needs and show us how to love them the way you love us. I pray specifically for my husband as he parents, that he would _____.

TAKE ACTION

* Offer to take over a parenting responsibility that is typically your husband's; give him the night off.

* Ask your husband how you could better support him in parenting the kids. Be open to his input.

CLAIM HIS PROMISES

In the fear of the LORD one has strong confidence,
and his children will have a refuge.
—PROVERBS 14:26 ESV

Love the Lord L-2:
A Spirit-empowered disciple listens to and hears God for daily decisions and direction for life.

Notes

A SPIRIT-EMPOWERED DISCIPLE

Lives
the Word

Day 11

CHEERING FOR ONE ANOTHER

Love God's Word and live it out by encouraging others.

STORIES FROM A WIFE'S HEART

I've decided to declare myself a cheerleader for my husband. With sincerity and genuine praise, I make a point to tell him at least once a week how much I believe in him. I cheer him on when things are hard at the office or when he's getting weary of the stress in his extended family. I call him on his big days at work. I text him just to remind him that I love him and that I'm praying for him. I show him that I believe in him by not taking over when he's caring for the kids or telling him how to do a job around the house. I make a special effort to speak confidently about his abilities in front of our friends and family.

Encouragement isn't just for hard times. It's not something to give as a last resort. Encouragement is continued gratitude for your husband. It means you share hope about your marriage with words such as, "Sweetheart, I'm so thankful that you and I were able to resolve our differences. It gives me confidence for the days ahead." It means that you share words of excitement about your future together: "Honey, you and I are good together. I can't wait to see what God does in our relationship in the future!"

PRAY: LISTEN TO JESUS

Come to me when you are discouraged or weary. Come closer to me when life is hard. I can give you rest. While you are in this world, there will be trouble, but take heart, I have overcome the troubles of this world. Remember too: I can fill you with joy and peace in the midst of the hard times. I am able to give you sufficiency and abundance for everything I have called you to do. (See Matthew 11:28; Romans 15:13; 2 Corinthians 9:8; John 16:33.)

* Jesus, thank you for being my encourager. I am weary at times, in _____, and I need your _____. Sometimes it's hard to keep going in _____, so I need your _____.

* Lord, I also pray that you lift up and encourage my husband. Give him rest in _____. Fill him with joy and peace in the midst of _____. Give him your sufficiency and abundance for _____.

LIVE: DO THE BIBLE

Encourage each other and build each other up, just as you are already doing.

—1 Thessalonians 5:11

* God, show me the areas where my husband might be weary. Show me the ways in which it might be hard for him to keep going. Help me to know exactly what encouragement he needs and how to communicate it. Speak to my heart, I am listening.

* Jesus, I pray for my husband. It seems as if it's hard for him to keep going in this area: _____. Help me build him up and cheer him forward. I think my husband needs to know that I believe he can _____. Help me communicate encouragement in ways that are meaningful to him.

TAKE ACTION

● Send your husband a note that begins with these words: *I know it's hard sometimes. I want you to know that I believe in you and your* _____.

● Ask your husband: "How can I best encourage you as you accomplish your goals this week?"

CLAIM HIS PROMISES

God is able to make all grace abound to you, so that always having all sufficiency in everything, you may have an abundance for every good deed.
— 2 Corinthians 9:8 nasb

Live the Word W-2:
A Spirit-empowered disciple lives the Word by demonstrating a love for God's Word and living it out every day.

Day 12

A DIVINE COMMODITY

Love God's Word and live it out, especially as you accept others.

STORIES FROM A WIFE'S HEART

My husband is so different from me. I am laid back, while he's punctual to the point of being compulsive about being on time. I'm flexible, and he's a perfectionist. I'm quiet and reserved; he's outgoing and likes lots of attention. When my life gets stressful, these differences between us can make my husband seem—from my perspective—impatient, critical, and loud. Those character traits are difficult for me to accept.

I have learned, however, that acceptance doesn't mean condoning someone's behavior. It simply means looking deeper than someone's actions to see that person's true worth, just as God does with me. Christ looked beyond Zacchaeus's selfishness and greed and offered kindness. Jesus separated Peter's impulsiveness from his worth. Christ talked with the woman at the well who lived year after year in habitual sin, and offered her freedom because He saw her need for love.

Have I ever been selfish or greedy? Undoubtedly. I've cheated my husband out of undivided attention and stolen his joy at times. Have I ever acted without thinking or spoken without caution? Absolutely. Are there sins I live with year after year? Yes. And yet, despite these imperfections and sins, God still accepts me.

As I look beyond my husband's differences, my gratitude for him continues to grow. But that happens only as I remind myself of how Christ accepts me despite my shortcomings.

PRAY: LISTEN TO JESUS

Acceptance is a divine commodity. It's only available from me. You must receive it before you can give it. When my Father allowed me to die in your place, He made a deliberate choice to look beyond your imperfections, inadequacies, and sin to accept you as you are. This unconditional acceptance is permanent. There is nothing you can do to earn it or lose it. Now I see you as one who is favored, righteous, and worth my blessings. (See Romans 5:8, 15:7; Psalm 5:12; Numbers 6:24–26.)

* Jesus, you loved me and died for me in spite of my _____. I am filled with gratitude for how you have looked beyond my _____. You see me as one who is favored and righteous even though I _____. Help me accept my husband as he is, focusing instead on the changes I need to make.

* Lord, I pray you would reassure my husband of your unconditional acceptance. Confirm to him that your love is not based on his _____ or _____. Speak to his heart about how you see him as favored, righteous, and worth

your blessings. Let him experience a fresh taste of your acceptance.

LIVE: DO THE BIBLE

Accept each other just as Christ has accepted you so that God will be given glory.
—ROMANS 15:7

* God, I want to accept my husband the way you have accepted me. Show me how you see him. I can sometimes only see our differences, disagreements, irritations, idiosyncrasies, or faults. Help me look beyond those, see him with your eyes, and respond with your love.

* Jesus, I pray that my husband would see me with your eyes. Help him see beyond my faults. Help him sense more of your acceptance and then empower him to give it to others.

TAKE ACTION

* Try this conversation starter. Keep it light-hearted and celebrate your differences. "Remember when we noticed that we were different in _____?"

* Write a note to your husband: *I'm grateful that you love me even though I _____.*

* If one of your husband's imperfections shows up, respond with, "We've all got some growing to do. But for me, you are perfect."

CLAIM HIS PROMISES

My grace is sufficient for you, for power is perfected in weakness.

—2 CORINTHIANS 12:9 HCSB

Live the Word W-2:
A Spirit-empowered disciple lives the Word by demonstrating a love for God's Word and living it out every day.

Day 13

TEARS OF COMFORT

Love God's Word and live it out, especially as you comfort others.

STORIES FROM A WIFE'S HEART

I have often wondered about the times when Christ withdrew from the crowds and spent time alone with the Father. I can't help but think that as Christ spent time with God, the Father showered compassion and love on His Son. I'm just certain that the Father spent some time comforting Jesus, telling Him how much He hurt that Christ was burdened by the cares of the world. It's those exchanges that must have empowered Jesus to have compassion on the multitudes. It seems that compassion follows comfort.

In order to have compassion for one another, we must first have received comfort for our pain. My friend brought her husband to see us after twelve years of marriage. She complained that he often seemed cold and callous toward her hurts. She knew he didn't intend to hurt her, but his tendency to minimize his own pain left him insensitive to his wife's. The wife told us that when her huband's mom died five years earlier, he had never really mourned her death even though they had been very close. She suggested that his inability to grieve was just one example of his calloused heart.

My husband and I suggested that the wife tell her husband how sad she felt over his loss and the loneliness he must feel, rather than pointing out his shortcomings. She held his hand and poured out her sorrow for him. He wept openly as years of pent-up grief flooded out. Over the next few months, as she continued to share words of comfort with her husband, he began to learn how to reciprocate. He became more sensitive and compassionate. God began to bless the wife with what she had longed for—more of her husband's heartfelt compassion.

PRAY: LISTEN TO JESUS

Just as I was moved with compassion for my Son, I hurt deeply when I see your sadness, disappointment, and hurt. I will never, ever leave you comfortless. My love, comfort, hope, strength, and grace are always available for you. I am the God of all comfort, so when you're called upon to give compassion to others, call on me. (See John 11:1–34, 14:8; 2 Corinthians 1:3–4.)

* Jesus, when I imagine that the Savior of the universe hurts for me, cries for me, and is moved with compassion for me, I feel _____. As I receive your care and comfort, let me share that with my husband when he needs it.

* Lord, I also pray that you would give my husband a personal experience of your divine compassion. I know he's felt hurt about _____ and needs some of your comfort.

LIVE: DO THE BIBLE

Weep with those who weep.

—ROMANS 12:15 NASB

* God, I know that my husband has experienced these hurts, disappointments, and pains: _____. Because I love him, it makes me sad to know that he has gone through these things.

* Jesus, please help me express some of your comfort to my husband. Bring healing to his heart.

TAKE ACTION

* If your husband shares a struggle or painful emotion, sit quietly and listen attentively.

* Share words of comfort with your husband:
   o "Sweetheart, I know you have felt _____, and I'm so sorry you're going through this."
   o "It makes me sad to hear you say _____, because I love you and don't want to see you hurting."

CLAIM HIS PROMISES

Show mercy and compassion for others, just as your heavenly Father overflows with mercy and compassion for all.

—LUKE 6:36 TPT

Live the Word W-2:
A Spirit-empowered disciple lives the Word by demonstrating a love for God's Word and living it out every day.

Day 14

GOOD FOR
THE SOUL

Love God's Word and live it out, especially as you confess your sins to others.

STORIES FROM A WIFE'S HEART

My husband and I hurt each other. We don't mean to, but we do. Unfortunately, those hurts don't simply go away on their own. Time doesn't spontaneously heal resentments. We need to confess the sin behind the hurt and ask each other for forgiveness.

It's sobering to realize that my selfishness, my unloving attitude, and my abusive words are the kinds of sin that sent Christ to the cross. Experiencing His redemption and forgiveness frees me to confess my sin to my husband and ask him to forgive me.

As God challenges me to look at how I've hurt my husband, and to grieve my hurtful actions, He also promises me that because He has forgiven me, it is safe for me to confess my sin to the person I love most. It's still hard for me to say, "Honey, I realize that my sharp tongue has hurt you. I was wrong. Please forgive me." But I know it is the first step to freedom. When he says back to me, "Thank you. And I forgive you," I feel cleansed.

I encourage you to practice confession and forgiveness with your husband. Take time alone to list ways in which you may have hurt each other. Ask yourself, *Have I been selfish, critical, negative, insensitive, disrespectful, verbally abusive, or unsupportive?* Take your list, confess each item to God, and receive His forgiveness. Finally, come back together, share your lists, and request forgiveness. Experience the freedom of forgiveness—from God and from your spouse.

PRAY: LISTEN TO JESUS

Confession is hard, but it has great reward. Your confession— admitting your wrong actions, attitudes, and behavior— keeps us in right relationship with one another. You have less worry, guilt, and anxiety when you practice confession with me. When you admit your sin, you can count on my forgiveness. It's a promise. Confessing to another person brings the promise of healing in that relationship too. (See 1 John 1:9; Psalm 38:18, 51:1-9; James 5:16; Lamentations 3:23.)

* God, I am grateful for your promise of forgiveness and how that keeps me close to you because _____. Thank you that I can empty my guilt, worry, and anxiety through confession.

* Lord, I pray that you would reassure my husband of your forgiveness. Overwhelm him with the truth that he can trust your lovingkindness to be new every morning.

LIVE: DO THE BIBLE

I acknowledged my sin to you,
And my iniquity I have not hidden.

—PSALM 32:5 NKJV

* God, search my heart and tell me if there are attitudes, behaviors, or habits (especially those that impact my husband) that are wrong in your sight and need my confession. Lord, I admit that I was wrong in _____. Will you forgive me for _____? Help me share these points of confession with my husband.

* God, I pray for my husband. Empower him to receive my confession and forgive. Would you bring more healing and restoration to our marriage?

TAKE ACTION

- Set aside a private time with your husband. Share the areas of confession that the Lord has revealed.

- Avoid excuses or defensiveness in your confession. A great confession sounds like:
  - "I was wrong when _____."
  - "I know you must have felt _____."
  - "Will you forgive me?"

CLAIM HIS PROMISES

Whoever conceals his transgressions will not prosper,
but he who confesses and forsakes them will obtain mercy.

—PROVERBS 28:13 ESV

Live the Word W-2:
A Spirit-empowered disciple lives the Word by demonstrating a love for God's Word and living it out every day.

Day 15

RELEASE
YOUR GRIP

Love God's Word and live it out, especially as you forgive others.

STORIES FROM A WIFE'S HEART

In Greek, the word for forgiveness means "to release." Before, when I forgave, I released the person and the action, but I failed to release my pain. I forgave, but I still felt hurt. I wasn't dealing with the pain associated with the offense.

It's been difficult, but I've discovered that I need to share my pain with the Lord. It's not enough just to "gut it out" and forgive my offender. The Lord wants to heal the hurt that I've endured, and that requires that I share it with Him. Jesus wants me to tell Him about my disappointment and let Him comfort me. He wants me to talk with Him about my rejection, so He can remind me He understands how deeply I hurt.

One important step in my experience of forgiveness is to imagine myself alone in the garden of Gethsemane with Jesus. I listen as He shares His hurt and pain with the Father. (See Matthew 26:36–46.)

Jesus shared His hurt with God, so it must be okay for me to do the same. I imagine the scene of the angels comforting my suffering Savior (Luke 22:43–44). I'm then free to tell the Father about my own painful experiences and wait until the God of all comfort pours His healing compassion over me. Finally, I reflect on how Jesus must have needed this time of healing and comfort with the Father so that He could offer forgiveness at the cross. In the same way, it is my experience of God's compassion and care that allows me to truly forgive.

PRAY: LISTEN TO JESUS

I am good, ready to forgive, and full of unfailing love for anyone who asks for my help. If someone has hurt you, I want to comfort you and help you forgive. Make allowances for other's faults. Forgive them and you will be forgiven. I know releasing is hard, but it's a matter of stewardship. My Father has granted you forgiveness, now it's your turn to share His gift with others. Remember, if you refuse to forgive, your Father will not forgive you. (See Matthew 6:15; Psalm 86:5; Luke 6:31; Colossians 3:13.)

* Jesus, I need your comfort for my hurt caused by _____. Help me to completely release my pain about _____. Bring more of your freedom and forgiveness into my life.

* Lord, I pray that you would do the same for my husband. Would you remind him of your readiness to help and comfort? Comfort the hurts he has about _____.

LIVE: DO THE BIBLE

Make allowance for each other's faults, and forgive anyone who offends you. Remember, the Lord forgave you, so you must forgive others.

—COLOSSIANS 3:13

* God, just as you have forgiven me, would you help me forgive _____? Help me make allowances for _____. I'm trusting the Holy Spirit to _____.

* Jesus, I pray that you would help my husband forgive _____. Help him make allowances for _____. Empower him to trust your Spirit as _____.

TAKE ACTION

* Write a letter to Jesus, telling Him about the hurts you've experienced and any areas of unforgiveness. Allow the Holy Spirit to bring you comfort, healing, and forgiveness for each moment of pain.

* After you have received comfort from the Lord and have a forgiving heart toward your offender, it may be time to share your hurt. That might sound like: "I need to share something that's been painful for me. I care about our relationship and want you to know that it was hurtful when _____ (name the incident without judgment). I felt _____ (name your hurt). Thank you for listening." Then leave the topic, trusting the Holy Spirit to bring confession and change.

CLAIM HIS PROMISES

> *Love prospers when a fault is forgiven,*
> *but dwelling on it separates close friends.*
>
> —PROVERBS 17:9

Live the Word W-2:

A Spirit-empowered disciple lives the Word by demonstrating a love for God's Word and living it out every day.

Day 16

BUILD HIM UP

Love God's Word and live it out, especially as you speak only words that edify others.

STORIES FROM A WIFE'S HEART

My husband and I have worked diligently on how we talk to each other. We've determined to speak only words that are wholesome and beneficial. First, I check to make sure that the purpose of my words is to build up or esteem him. If my purpose is to hurt, attack, or defend my position, then it's not time for me to talk.

Second, I must discern the need. Ephesians 4:29 says to only speak words that fit the need of the moment. This is why it is important that I listen to my husband. Is he sad? Then I'll want to show him how much I care. Is he insecure? Then I'll want to reassure him of my love and presence. Is he angry about something I've done? Then I'll want to ask the Lord to convict me of any way I might have hurt him.

Third, I try to make sure the timing of my words is right. My husband's receptivity to my words is often directly related to the timing of my speaking them. For example, I've learned that it's rarely a good idea to talk with him about something important late at night, so we usually have our talks early in the morning over coffee. We've also found that bringing up important issues during our weekly marriage staff meetings works well. We both know that those times are dedicated to giving one another undivided attention.

PRAY: LISTEN TO JESUS

When I look at you, I celebrate the specialness of you, my creation. Scripture reveals how I'm generous with my edifying words for you. You are my chosen one. You are my masterpiece, the light of the world, holy, blameless, and complete. I want you to have this same view of the people around you. Look for their special qualities and build them up. Think carefully before saying anything that's critical or dishonoring. My followers are careful to only speak words that edify. (See Proverbs 15:28; Ephesians 1:4; 2:10, 4:29; Colossians 1:22.)

* God, I'm grateful for your words of edification for me. Thank you for reminding me that you see me as _____. I'm blessed by the truth that you have called me _____.

* Lord, I pray that my husband would see himself as you see him. Remind him often of the truth that he is _____. Because of your grace, you have called him _____.

LIVE: DO THE BIBLE

Do not let any unwholesome talk come out of your mouths, but only what is helpful for building others up according to their needs, that it may benefit those who listen.

—Ephesians 4:29 niv

* God, make me generous with praise for my husband. What words of edification are most important for him to hear from me? What words of criticism or comparison do I need to get rid of? I want him to only hear words that are honoring.

* Lord, I pray that my husband would live out the command of Ephesians 4:29. Empower his generosity of praise. Give him words that are edifying, not critical or comparative.

TAKE ACTION

● After the Lord has reminded you of the positive character traits that are true of your husband, share those with him privately through a text, note, or verbally. "I'm so proud that you're my husband because of your _____."

● Brag on your husband in front of his parents, friends, or kids. Build him up in public settings.

CLAIM HIS PROMISES

As the bridegroom rejoices over the bride, so your God will rejoice over you.

—ISAIAH 62:5 NIV

Live the Word W-2:
A Spirit-empowered disciple lives the Word by demonstrating a love for God's Word and living it out every day.

Day 17

PRIORITIZING
PREFERENCES

Love God's Word and live it out, especially as you give preference to others.

STORIES FROM A WIFE'S HEART

Hurts, irritations, and unmet needs—life is full of them. How ironic it is that marriage often magnifies these. For example, you might quickly forget if a casual friend shows a lack of interest in your conversation; you probably think nothing of it. But if your husband fails to give you undivided attention, look out!

For many years, I applied a simple but flawed approach to understanding my husband's reactions and preferences to certain situations. My approach was to ask these questions: "If the same thing that happened to him happened to me, would I react the way he is reacting?" "Are his objections or preferences valid or similar to mine?" The way I saw it, if I would not have been disappointed or hurt, then he should not be either. Because of this, I was not tender in my responses to his hurts, so there was little or no caring connection between us. In fact, my responses only made matters worse.

Over time, the Holy Spirit pierced my heart with this painful and convicting truth: "This is not about you; it's about him and his pain. Will you let me care for him through you? I gave up my preference of heaven for a relationship with you. There are times when I am asking you to do the same for your husband."

PRAY: LISTEN TO JESUS

Remember, my beloved. I had equal status with my heavenly Father, but I didn't cling to that position. I exchanged my status and the privileges of deity and became human. I did this for you! I gave up myself and gave preference to you and to our relationship. I want this same kind of selflessness to be true of you. Give preference to your husband. Love deeply. Trust in me and I will lift you up. (See Romans 12:10; Philippians 2:1–11; 1 Peter 5:6.)

* Jesus, I am grateful for your demonstration of humility and how you gave preference to me because _____. I feel _____ when I imagine that you gave up your position in heaven so you could have a relationship with me.

* Lord, I pray that you would plant this same truth deeply into my husband's heart. Give him a fresh experience of how you have sacrificed and given yourself up for him. I pray specifically that he would sense your _____.

LIVE: DO THE BIBLE

Give preference to one another in honor.

—ROMANS 12:10 NASB

* God, I want to give preference to my husband. Show me the ways I can give myself up for him. Speak to me, Lord, about when to give up my agenda, preferences, and privileges. Help me do this with a positive attitude and servant spirit.

* Lord, I pray that my husband would sense this same need. Move his heart with this same stewardship and servant's heart. You gave up yourself for us, and we are now called to do the same for others.

TAKE ACTION

● Ask your husband about his preferences—at home, with the kids, about schedules, traditions, etc. Discuss those preferences and then focus on your giving. Trust the Lord to meet your needs through your husband in His timing and in His ways.

● Ask your husband to share his responses to this statement: "In our marriage, I would prefer more or less _____. It would mean a lot to me if we could _____."

CLAIM HIS PROMISES

Do nothing out of selfish ambition or vain conceit. Rather, in humility value others above yourselves.

—PHILIPPIANS 2:3 NIV

Live the Word W-2:
A Spirit-empowered disciple lives the Word by demonstrating a love for God's Word and living it out every day.

Notes

A SPIRIT-
EMPOWERED
DISCIPLE

Loves

People

Day 18

STAMP
OF APPROVAL

Discern the relational needs of others and share God's love in meaningful
ways, especially as you speak words of approval.

STORIES FROM A WIFE'S HEART

Approval means thinking and speaking well of others. It means commending someone because of who they are, apart from what they do. It means affirming the importance of a relationship. It's helpful to remember how the Father met the Son's need for approval.

Jesus was standing in line with the rest of the followers waiting to be baptized. John the Baptist raised his hand and announced that Jesus of Nazareth was to be baptized that day. As Jesus came out of the water, the heavens opened up and the Spirit of God descended like a dove. Out of nowhere, a thundering voice announced, "This is my beloved Son, in whom I am well pleased" (Matthew 3:17 ESV).

With these simple words, the heavenly Father was essentially bragging about His Son. It's also important to notice that the Father initiated this contact. Jesus didn't have to ask for it. And one final thing to notice: The Father approved of His Son before the Son had done anything. This blessing came before Jesus had performed any miracles, healed, or converted anyone. The Father gave His Son approval because of who He was, not for what He had done. As the Father approved of the Son, so He approves of you.

PRAY: LISTEN TO JESUS

I love you for who you are apart from what you do. You don't have to do anything to earn my love. My love for you is unconditional. I know everything there is to know about you, your strengths, and your weaknesses, and still, it was the possibility of a relationship with you that brought me to Calvary. You are my beloved, you are chosen. I am pleased with you, and you are one in whom I delight. (See Matthew 3:17; Exodus 33:17; Ephesians 1:7; 1 John 3:1.)

* Jesus, when I reflect on how you love me apart from what I do, I feel grateful because _____. In considering that you endured Calvary because a relationship with me was important to you, I am moved with feelings of _____.

* Lord, I pray that my husband would sense this same approval from you. Give him a fresh experience of affirming love. Reassure my husband that you love him apart from what he does.

LIVE: DO THE BIBLE

Commend those who do right.

—1 Peter 2:14 niv

* God, show me some of the ways I can give words of approval and commendation to my husband. What character traits should I affirm in him? Show me what you see in him. I want him to sense my pride because _____.

* God, I pray that my husband would see more and more opportunities to affirm, approve, and commend others. Would you reveal positive aspects of the character of others and empower him to verbalize them?

TAKE ACTION

• Do an internet search for a list of positive character traits. Choose two traits that are true about your husband each week. Share them verbally or in writing: "I am proud you are my husband because you are _____. I see that trait in you when _____."

• Post your husband's photo in your office. Brag on him often in front of your coworkers.

• Look for opportunities to openly admire your husband. "I am so impressed with my husband. He is an amazing _____ (man/father/husband/provider) because _____."

CLAIM HIS PROMISES

"Give, and it will be given to you."

—LUKE 6:38 NASB

Love People P-3:
A Spirit-empowered disciple loves people by discerning relational needs of others and sharing God's love in meaningful ways.

Day 19

CLOSENESS THROUGH TOUCH

Discern the relational needs of others and share God's love in meaningful ways, especially as you give them affection.

STORIES FROM A WIFE'S HEART

The ancient wisdom of Solomon provides contemporary insight into relationships. Ecclesiastes 3:5 says that there is an appointed time to embrace one another. In a world filled with the barrenness of busy lives, taking time to give affection to your husband may seem so simple that you can mistakenly conclude it is insignificant.

To demonstrate affection means leaving love notes, holding hands, and calling just because you want to hear his voice. Affection means doing the simple things that stoke the fires of attraction. It means enticing your spouse, gaining his favor, and, as Solomon suggests, embracing him. And yes, sometimes it includes sex.

To embrace my husband seemed so common and simplistic in years past. What I realized, though, is that there's often no better demonstration of intimacy than putting my arms around the one I love. To embrace—to give a hug—isn't just a polite sign of welcome. It's also an affirmation of my husband's worth and a declaration that I value the relationship.

PRAY: LISTEN TO JESUS

My love for you is an everlasting love; I want you to experience how wide, long, high, and deep it is. Imagine it's evening and you are sitting safely on a boat in the middle of the ocean. The sea is perfectly calm, and the stars are shining brightly. My love is like the horizon. It doesn't end; you just can't see it all at once. My love is higher than the stars; you'll never be able to reach its limits. My love goes on forever; there are no time constraints or expiration dates. My love is deeper than the ocean floor; you'll never reach its end. I love you with an everlasting love. (See Isaiah 42:6; Jeremiah 31:3; 1 John 3:1; Ephesians 3:18.)

* Jesus, when I imagine that your care for me never ends, my heart is moved with gratitude because _____. When I reflect on your limitless and everlasting love, I am in awe of you because _____.

* Lord, I pray that my husband would sense the vastness of your love for him. Would you overwhelm him in a new way with the height, the depth, and the extent of your love, especially as he _____?

LIVE: DO THE BIBLE

Greet one another with a holy kiss.

—ROMANS 16:16 NASB

* God, I want to communicate affection and closeness to my husband through my tender words and gentle touch. Help me know the right words to say because _____. Help me know the right time and the meaningful ways to communicate my love for him, especially as _____.

* Lord, I pray that you would empower my husband to share his love through tender words and gentle touch. Help him share more and more of your love through _____.

TAKE ACTION

• Surprise your husband by going out of your way to creatively communicate that you love him. Write a love note that says, *I was thinking of you _____,* or *You are important to me because _____.*

• Make a sixty-second phone call during the day and say, "Hi, Sweetheart. I was just calling to say I love you. See you tonight. Bye."

• Leave your husband in the morning with a tender hug and kiss. Greet him when you arrive home with this same demonstration of closeness. Initiate sex.

CLAIM HIS PROMISES

No one has seen God, ever. But if we love one another, God dwells deeply within us, and his love becomes complete in us—perfect love!

—1 JOHN 4:12 MSG

Love People P-3:
A Spirit-empowered disciple loves people by discerning relational needs of others and sharing God's love in meaningful ways.

Day 20

GRATITUDE AND APPRECIATION

Discern the relational needs of others and share God's love in meaningful ways, especially as you appreciate them.

STORIES FROM A WIFE'S HEART

Isn't it a great feeling to be appreciated for something you've done? There is hardly anything like it. A verbal pat on the back when something is done well is encouraging and sometimes even necessary. When others notice your effort and give you verbal praise that is clear, strong, and accurate, you know beyond a doubt that you are being appreciated. Genuine appreciation is unselfish; it's an expression of gratitude for the benefit of others.

One important element in true appreciation is the ability to demonstrate that you genuinely know someone. If I were to appreciate my husband for his careful attention to detail in loading the dishwasher, he would either laugh or wonder if I had lost my mind. Attention to detail is definitely not one of his strengths, and it would not be genuine if I were to praise him for it. On the other hand, he would be blessed if I were to express my gratitude for his commitment to provide for our family, the way he researches big purchases so that we get the best deal, or how hard he works in our yard. These words of praise would affirm that I really do know him. Praise your husband for the things he does and the effort he makes. Don't let your marriage be deficient in appreciation.

PRAY: LISTEN TO JESUS

I am a God who sees. I see all your steps, I see all that you do and the effort you make, and I intercede on your behalf. You can count on me and my great name; I won't leave you or abandon you in the midst of all you do. (See Genesis 16:13; Job 34:21; Romans 8:27.)

* Jesus, it makes me so grateful to know that you are a God who sees because _____. I am thankful that you notice the things I do and that you intercede for me because _____. I'm grateful I can count on you to be with me in the midst of _____.

* Jesus, would you let my husband know that you see how he _____? Reassure him that you know and acknowledge his_____ even when I miss it.

LIVE: DO THE BIBLE

I thank my God always concerning you.

—1 Corinthians 1:4 nasb

* God, would you show me the things my husband does that may go unnoticed or that I take for granted? Empower me to take initiative and tell him and the world about how

much he does for me and for our family. I'm especially grateful today for how he _____.

* Lord, would you give my husband the special vision to see the things that others do and the effort they make? Empower him to speak up and say thank you often.

TAKE ACTION

● Appreciate your husband in front of family or friends: "I want you to know that my husband is a very special man. He is amazing. He does so much for our family like _____."

● Bring home a special gift, a thoughtfully composed letter, or a treat as a demonstration of your appreciation.

● Share these words with your husband: "I'm so grateful for you and how you _____."

CLAIM HIS PROMISES

The LORD remembers us and will bless us.

—PSALM 115:12 HCSB

Love People P-3:
A Spirit-empowered disciple loves people by discerning relational needs of others and sharing God's love in meaningful ways.

Day 21

ENTERING ANOTHER'S WORLD

Discern the relational needs of others and share God's love in meaningful ways, especially as you give them attention.

STORIES FROM A WIFE'S HEART

I completed a painful assessment the other day. I asked myself how I was doing at meeting my husband's need for attention—more specifically, his need for me to listen. Do I give him individual, undivided, and unlimited attention?

Individual Attention: Do I purposefully talk and listen to him when we are alone? Just being in the house by ourselves doesn't count. In order to give individual attention, I must actively pursue a conversation with him—when no one else is around—and be a willing participant.

Undivided Attention: Do I make an effort to try to talk with him away from any potential interruptions? Do I concentrate on the conversation, or do I daydream or disengage? Do I dominate the conversation or encourage him to talk about his day?

Unlimited Attention: Does my husband sense my willingness to give plenty of time to discuss difficult subjects, or do I give off signals that I just want to get to the point? Does listening to him include a caring heart and loving attitude or just lots of advice and criticism?

After doing such an assessment, I was sobered by the results. I realized there were improvements that needed to be made in my life.

PRAY: LISTEN TO JESUS

I have set my love upon you. I will set you on high because I know your name. You will call upon me, and I will hear you. I will be with you in trouble; I will deliver you and honor you. Remember, I lean in to listen to the needs of your heart. The thoughts I have about you are precious, rare, and beautiful. I think about you so often, you couldn't even begin to count the times; they outnumber the sand of the seas. (See Psalm 4:3, 91:14–15, 139:17–18.)

* Jesus, it amazes me that you lean in and listen to me. I'm calling upon you today and trusting that you will hear me about _____. You are attentive to me and my world and I give you thanks because _____.

* Lord, I pray that my husband would come to a new understanding of how attentive you are to his needs. Would you reassure him that you listen? Remind him of your attentiveness and thoughtfulness even when I miss the mark.

LIVE: DO THE BIBLE

That the members may have the same care for one another.

—1 Corinthians 12:25 nasb

* God, show me how to care for my husband and give him my attention. In what ways do I need to listen to him more effectively and understand him more deeply? What things can we enjoy doing together that are part of his world?

* Lord, I pray that my husband would enjoy your attentiveness and then be more free to give to others. Reveal new ways that he can listen, understand, and enjoy giving to others as he enters their world.

TAKE ACTION

• Ask your husband about his day, and be prepared to listen.

• Watch a movie, try a hobby, or go to an event that purely appeals to your husband's interests.

• Say some of these sentences and be ready to follow through: "Let's do what you want to do tonight" or "I'd like to hear about some of your dreams and goals."

CLAIM HIS PROMISES

You faithfully answer our prayers with awesome deeds,
O God our savior.

—Psalm 65:5

Love People P-3:

A Spirit-empowered disciple loves people by discerning relational needs of others and sharing God's love in meaningful ways.

Day 22

HONOR AND VALUE

Discern the relational needs of others and share God's love in meaningful ways, especially as you show them respect.

STORIES FROM A WIFE'S HEART

Giving respect means that my heart is yielded to the Holy Spirit's work. It means there are times when I am willing to give up my agenda, my preferences, and my schedule for the benefit of someone else. Respect means that my needs are not always my top priority. Respecting my husband means that I submit myself to God and then become aware of and care about my husband's needs.

Respect is never a one-way street, nor is it relinquishing all my desires and becoming a doormat. God intends for each of us to give respect as well as receive it.

I finally began to see the wisdom of respecting my husband's impressions concerning our kids. I was sure that the kids needed more structure and routine. He believed that they needed more experiences of adventure and fun. At first, I was reluctant to accept his impressions, but the Holy Spirit challenged me to respect him, knowing that he too was hearing from the Lord. Our home environment changed dramatically after I had implemented several of his suggestions. Our home was less conflicted *and* more fun!

Finally, I've realized it's impossible to maintain a submissive attitude in marriage apart from first yielding to the Holy Spirit's work.

PRAY: LISTEN TO JESUS

I place great value on our relationship; in fact, I call you my friend. I chose you and appointed you, that you should go and bear fruit and bring honor to my name. Remember that when you call on me, I will rescue you and honor you because I love you. Before honor comes humility, so make sure that you see others as more important than yourself. Give honor to all people. (See John 15:15–16; Psalm 91:15; Proverbs 18:12; Philippians 2:3; 1 Peter 2:17.)

* Jesus, I feel respected that you call me your friend because _____. When I imagine that you have chosen and appointed me, I feel grateful for this honor because _____.

* Lord, I pray that you would remind my husband that you have chosen him. You have appointed him to be your friend. This is a divine honor. Would you help him embrace and experience all that this means for him, especially as he _____?

LIVE: DO THE BIBLE

Be devoted to one another in brotherly love. Honor one another above yourselves.

—ROMANS 12:10 NIV

* God, would you show me new ways I can honor and respect my husband. In what ways can I defer to him and let go of my preferences? Show me topics that need his input, ideas, and feedback. In what ways do I need to think more highly of him than I do myself? I know he needs my respect in these areas: _____.

* Lord, I pray that you would empower my husband to give honor to _____. Help him show respect in this area: _____. Enable him to think more highly of _____ in this way: _____.

TAKE ACTION

* Ask your husband, "You're so good at helping me think through things. What do you think I should do about _____?" or "Your opinion is really important to me, so what's your opinion about _____?"

* Arrive on time for events that are important to your husband. Keep spending within the family budget and honor financial agreements. Listen to his perspective and ask for his ideas.

CLAIM HIS PROMISES

> *The wise are promoted to honor, but fools are promoted to shame!*
>
> —PROVERBS 3:35 TLB

Love People P-3:
A Spirit-empowered disciple loves people by discerning relational needs of others and sharing God's love in meaningful ways.

Day 23

BEARING THE LOAD

Discern the relational needs of others and share God's love in meaningful ways, especially as you support them.

STORIES FROM A WIFE'S HEART

When our kids were very young, I got overstressed when I was put in situations where I had to referee conflicts between my husband and the children. He learned to support me by talking about any of his concerns out of earshot of the kids first. He got stressed when work required that he travel for weeks at a time. I learned to support him by helping him pack, getting the kids to pitch in extra time around the house, and calling him every evening just to relationally connect.

We learned that we really could navigate the stressful times of life when we were vulnerable with our needs for support and had some prevention plans in place. First, we identified the things that triggered stress for each of us when we were calm and not in the middle of the craziness. Then we made plans for reducing stress before the craziness hit again.

Last, we implemented another dimension of support for each other. We identified the things that each of us needs when it's time for an escape, and then lovingly insisted on those times. When the kids were too much for me, he lovingly insisted that I go to lunch or walk with my friends. When things were too much for him, I lovingly insisted that he go to the gym or call his buddies for a game of golf. Bearing the load can sometimes mean helping my husband hit a load of golf balls and let off a little steam.

PRAY: LISTEN TO JESUS

I will accomplish what concerns you. My lovingkindness is everlasting, so I will not forsake the works of my hands. I will equip you with everything good, so you are able to do the things I have called you to do, the work which is pleasing in my sight. As you receive my care and support, be sure to offer the same to others. When you carry their burdens, you're living out my commands. (See Psalm 138:8; Hebrews 13:20–21; Galatians 6:2.)

* Jesus, when I read your words and know that you will accomplish what concerns me, I am thankful because _____. To know that you have equipped me with everything I need to do the work you've called me to do makes me incredibly grateful because _____.

* Lord, remind my husband that he has been equipped by the living God for _____. You have promised to accomplish _____. You have called him to _____, and you will not forsake the work of your hands.

LIVE: DO THE BIBLE

Carry each other's burdens, and in this way you will fulfill the law of Christ.
—GALATIANS 6:2 NIV

* God, show me ways that I can help share in my husband's burdens. How can I help relieve the burden of his to-do list, emotions that are heavy, or concerns of the heart? Show me practical ways I can pitch in and bring relief.

* Lord, empower my husband to receive support from you and then look for ways to give to others. Help him see opportunities to bear other people's burdens and fulfill your command.

TAKE ACTION

* Take initiative to help out with household chores that are typically your husband's responsibility. Ask, "Is there anything else I can do to shorten your list?"

* Say to your husband, "I'm committed to work alongside you and get this done" and "Could we take a few minutes and pray together about this?"

CLAIM HIS PROMISES

It is more blessed to give than to receive.
—ACTS 20:35

Love People P-3:
A Spirit-empowered disciple loves people by discerning relational needs of others and sharing God's love in meaningful ways.

Day 24

SAFE AND SECURE

Discern the relational needs of others and share God's love in meaningful ways, especially as you reassure them and bring security to your relationship.

STORIES FROM A WIFE'S HEART

Wisdom actually leads to security. But you can't touch, count, or even see wisdom. How could it possibly bring security? God knows that as you seek His wisdom and place your trust in what He values, you'll walk on secure ground.

My husband and I used to be one of those couples who were deceived into thinking that security comes from possessions. God told us that's not great wisdom: "Let not the wise man boast in his wisdom, let not the mighty man boast in his might, let not the rich man boast in his riches, but let him who boasts boast in this, that he understands and knows [God]" (Jeremiah 9:23–24 ESV). God wanted us to realize that possessions fade away but He can provide true safety from harm.

We used to be a couple who thought our marriage was immune to trouble because of our sexual passion and attraction to one another. God's wisdom says, "Charm is deceptive, and beauty is fleeting" (Proverbs 31:30 NIV). He wanted us to realize that beauty and human passions fade; it's only He who can provide unfailing love.

The first chapter of Proverbs reminded us that the voice of wisdom calls out to us. She has an incredible promise: "Whoever listens to me will live in safety and be at ease, without fear of harm" (32-33 NIV).

PRAY: LISTEN TO JESUS

I promise to never leave you or forsake you. I will always meet your needs. I will be your ever-present help in times of trouble. You can count on me to be faithful, unchangeable, and constant. I give security for those who trust in me as their Savior. The mountains may be removed and the hills may shake, but my lovingkindness will not be removed. My promise of peace will not be shaken. I will set you securely on high and protect you fiercely because you have known my name. (See Psalm 46:1; Lamentations 3:23; Hebrews 13:8; John 10:28; Isaiah 54:10; Psalm 91:14–15.)

* Jesus, I'm grateful for your reassurance about _____. I'm thankful for how you have given me security that _____. I am counting on you to _____.

* Lord, give my husband an extra dose of your security and protection. Reassure him that _____. Remind him that you are his ever-present help and unchangeable stability when _____.

LIVE: DO THE BIBLE

God has not given us a spirit of fear.

—2 Timothy 1:7 NIV

* God, I want to be a source of your security for my husband. In what ways can I give him reassurance and stability? What does he need most from me at this time? Speak, Lord. I want to hear from you.

* Lord, I pray that you would empower my husband to be a source of your security as well. Show him opportunities to give reassurance and stability to others.

TAKE ACTION

● Say these things to your husband, "I love you and I'll always love you, no matter what," "If I had to do it all over again, you're the one I would choose to spend my life with," and "I'm committed to you and to our marriage."

● Meet your husband's financial needs by living within the agreed-upon budget through careful planning.

● Meet his relational security needs by never referencing divorce or separation, or comparing him to other men.

CLAIM HIS PROMISES

"Love each other. Just as I have loved you, you should love each other."

—John 13:34

Love People P-3:
A Spirit-empowered disciple loves people by discerning relational needs of others and sharing God's love in meaningful ways.

Notes

A SPIRIT-
EMPOWERED
DISCIPLE

Lives His

Mission

Day 25

RECEIVE IT
THEN SHARE IT

Actively share your life with others and tell them about the Jesus who lives in you as you live a grace-filled life in front of them.

STORIES FROM A WIFE'S HEART

No doubt you know the parable of the prodigal son. It goes something like this: Kid takes trust fund and blows it on wine, women, and song; winds up in pig sty; and then returns home to beg for food and employment.

The most gripping scene in this biblical account is the father waiting for his wayward son. There is yearning on the father's face and anxiety mixed with anticipation. Then one day, the father glances toward the road and sees his son.

Reflect for a moment on your life. Have you had any "pig sty" moments? Have there been times when you were sure the Lord had had it with you, when you were scared that even begging His forgiveness wouldn't help? I certainly have. There have been plenty of times when I've just flat-out blown it badly.

Reconnect with your feelings during your prodigal moments: ashamed, sad, guilty, insecure, lost, anxious, and disconnected. Now picture the scene of the prodigal—you—coming home. You're coming down the road toward home. What do you see? It's your Father, and He's running toward you with outstretched arms. His face is relieved rather than strained or angry. He reaches you, embraces you, and holds you close to tell you how much He loves you. He's proud to call you His child. He's excited to see you. His love is unending and unwavering.

What feelings would that prompt in you? Gratefulness? Amazement? Humility? That is grace: a loving Father affirming the importance of the relationship with you in spite of your behavior.

PRAY: LISTEN TO JESUS

I couldn't bear the thought of heaven without you, so I gave you the ultimate gift. Remember, my gift of grace is new every morning; it never runs out. I'm available every moment to help you carry life's burdens and meet its challenges. Experience and receive my grace, honor me with your thanks, and then share my grace with others. (See Lamentations 3:23; Psalm 50:23, 68:19; 1 Peter 4:10.)

* Jesus, I am grateful your grace is new every morning because I need more of your _____ today. Would you infuse me with a fresh dose of your _____ for my husband?

* Lord, I pray that my husband would experience a new gift of your _____. Would you infuse him with a fresh dose of your _____ for me?

LIVE: DO THE BIBLE

As each one has received a special gift, employ it in serving one another as good stewards of the manifold grace of God.

—1 PETER 4:10 NASB

* God, I have received your gift of _____ and now I want to give it to my husband. I also want to share the hope that is in me with someone else. Who needs to hear about your grace and how it has empowered me to give?

* Lord, I pray that you would show my husband the person who might need to hear his story of God's grace and how it has empowered him.

TAKE ACTION

• Talk to your husband about the ways you have both received God's grace and how it has empowered your giving to one another. Pray together about who might need to hear your story.

CLAIM HIS PROMISES

I can do all things through him who strengthens me.

—PHILIPPIANS 4:13 ESV

Live His Mission M-1:

A Spirit-empowered disciple lives His mission by actively sharing their life with others and telling about the Jesus who lives inside of them.

Day 26

THE ZACCHAEUS PRINCIPLE

Actively share your life with others and tell them about the Jesus who lives in you, specifically as He empowers you to look beyond faults and see needs.

STORIES FROM A WIFE'S HEART

Zacchaeus—a hated tax collector, a traitor to his own people, and a thief—was no doubt often ridiculed and attacked for his sins. Lonely and curious, he climbed a tree to get a good look at the Messiah. He had to wonder if Jesus would notice him. And if He did, would He also reject him? (See Luke 19:1–10.)

What a miracle Christ's call must have been to this outcast! Our Savior asked Zacchaeus to share a meal, inviting him into one of the most intimate social settings of the day. This simple invitation from Jesus was a deliberate offer of welcome, reception, and loving relationship. Jesus looked beyond the faults of Zacchaeus and saw his need.

In the midst of Zacchaeus's failures, Jesus offered compassion, companionship, and acceptance. It's interesting to note what Jesus didn't do that day: He didn't attack the tax collector's behavior, point out things that were wrong with him, or even give helpful advice. He didn't remind Zacchaeus of what he should be doing or criticize him for not taking more responsibility. He didn't quote Scripture or make comparisons with other tax collectors. He didn't try to manipulate change in Zacchaeus or withhold affection from him.

My husband and I have experienced the blessing of the Zacchaeus Principle—to look beyond our partner's faults and see his or her needs. It doesn't go well for us to attack one another, point out things that are wrong, criticize, compare, manipulate, or withhold. Instead, we ask God for a fresh reminder of how He has looked beyond *our* faults and then ask for His help to do the same for others.

PRAY: LISTEN TO JESUS

I came to seek and to save you! I didn't wait until you shaped up or acted right. I looked beyond your faults and loved you while you were still a sinner. The world needs my kind of love; there's too much comparison, criticism, and selfishness. Look for opportunities to share how my love for you has changed your relationship with your husband. (See Luke 19:1–10; Romans 5:8.)

* Jesus, when I reflect on how you have looked past my faults and met my needs, I am filled with gratitude because _____. God, would you remind me of the awesome deeds you have done in my life and my marriage, particularly in how you have allowed me to look beyond faults and see needs?

* Lord, I pray that you would give my husband a fresh experience of gratitude for how you have changed our relationship. Give him insight into how you have empowered us to look beyond one another's faults to see and meet needs.

LIVE: DO THE BIBLE

Come and see the works of God,
who is awesome in His deeds
toward the sons of men.

—Psalm 66:5 NASB

* God, as I have come to have your same perspective with my husband and our marriage, I am grateful you have changed me and our relationship by _____. I'm thankful because _____. Who needs to hear and see your works? Give me opportunities to share your deeds.

* Lord, I pray you would remind my husband of what you have done in him and in our marriage. Give him opportunities to tell about your deeds.

TAKE ACTION

● Talk with your husband about how the Zacchaeus Principle has been true for you. Look for opportunities to share your story with others.

CLAIM HIS PROMISES

> *I pray that the sharing of your faith may become effective for the full knowledge of every good thing that is in us for the sake of Christ.*

—PHILEMON 1:6 ESV

Live His Mission M-1:

A Spirit-empowered disciple lives His mission by actively sharing their life with others and telling them about the Jesus who lives inside of them.

Day 27

SACRIFICE

Actively share your life with others and tell them about the Jesus who lives in you, especially as you are vulnerable with your weaknesses and struggles.

STORIES FROM A WIFE'S HEART

Love is not real love without sacrifice, without giving of oneself. Life would be empty had God not provided an example of sacrificial love when He gave up His own Son for the world. He made the ultimate sacrifice for humankind, providing an example of the blessing received in giving.

Receiving is where the human focus tends to be. Everyone has a measure of self-centeredness. Such focus can be related to the fear that, "Unless I look after me, no one will." Many struggle with self-centeredness in marriage.

To genuinely give consideration to another's ideas, feelings, and needs, I must be willing to lay aside my own. Many times I've asked my husband how he wants to spend a free afternoon, hoping all the while that we would do what I wanted. That's not exactly showing real consideration, is it? Focusing on his needs requires sacrifice, but it can also bring inexpressible joy. It gives God the opportunity to bring forth the greater blessing that comes in the giving of myself.

Giving consideration does not mean that I can't have ideas, feelings, and needs of my own. But I know that God will look after me as I put my husband's desires ahead of my own. God can be trusted to take what I have given, press it down, shake it together, and give it back to me overflowing (Luke 6:38).

PRAY: LISTEN TO JESUS

You can put your trust in me. I am faithful, and I am trustworthy in all I do. I am so trustworthy that I am surrounded by faithfulness. When you don't know what to do or you don't know where to turn, come to me. Let your eyes and focus be on me. I am your source. I have enough. As we walk together through the struggles of this world, we'll show others what it looks like to be my disciple. When you love one another even when it's hard, people will become convinced that I am the source of love. (See 2 Corinthians 1:18–20; Psalm 33:4; 89:8; 1 Peter 3:15.)

* Jesus, I am grateful that I can trust you to _____. I don't know what to do about _____, so my eyes are on you.

* Lord, remind my husband that you are faithful and he can trust you to _____. Please give him a renewed focus on you, so he knows what to do about _____.

LIVE: DO THE BIBLE

If someone asks about your hope as a believer, always be ready to explain it.

—1 PETER 3:15

* God, I want to share about my hope and trust in you. Empower me to be vulnerable about my struggle with _____ and how I am trusting you to _____. I have hope in you about _____, so give me the words and the opportunity to share this hope with those who don't yet know you.

* Lord, would you give my husband opportunities to share his story of hope with others? He is trusting you to _____, so give him the words to share with those who don't yet know you.

TAKE ACTION

* Talk with your husband about the struggles you have had in the past and how your trust in God brought healing, resolution, or peace. Pray together, asking for opportunities to share your testimony of hope with others.

CLAIM HIS PROMISES

Depend on God and keep at it because in the Lord God you have a sure thing.

—Isaiah 26:4 MSG

Live His Mission M-1:
A Spirit-empowered disciple lives His mission by actively sharing their life with others and telling them about the Jesus who lives inside of them.

Day 28

ONE OF A KIND

Actively share your life with others and tell them about the Jesus who lives
in you, specifically as you seize opportunities that arise in your daily life.

STORIES FROM A WIFE'S HEART

There isn't a sport that my husband doesn't like to watch or play—
any game, any time. He loves the action and the adrenaline. God
has blessed him with a passion for sports and an ability to coach
and play a few of them.

I am the opposite. I couldn't care less about games. I'd much
rather be repainting, retiling, or re-stenciling something. I'll go into
any house in the city and try my decorating magic.

Here's the amazing thing my husband and I have discovered
about our vastly different interests. My passion for decorating and
his interest in sports have allowed us to develop special friendships
with people who need Jesus. What once was an area of conflict
between us is now an opportunity to reach people for Christ. Some
weekends, I go to other people's homes to help them redo a bath-
room or repaint a bedroom. By the time I leave, I've developed

enough of a friendship that I invite them to our house to watch the next NFL or NBA game. When game time comes, we invite that couple, plus a few Jesus-followers, to our home and continue the relationship. It's been amazing. We're seeing friends come to Christ *because* of our different interests and passions!

PRAY: LISTEN TO JESUS

I've formed you with unique talents, interests, and abilities. I created you with these gifts so that you can be a one-of-a-kind expression of me. I placed all these abilities in you so that you can do the great things I have planned—like introduce others to me. I love to see you live out your interests and enjoy life, and I love seeing you bring my hope to this world. (See Colossians 1:27.)

* Jesus, when I imagine that you created me to be a one-of-a-kind expression of you and that you gave me these gifts to draw others to you, I feel _____.

* Lord, remind my husband of how he is a one-of-a-kind expression of you and how he is uniquely called to draw others to you with his gifts. Give him a renewed sense of your calling as he _____.

LIVE: DO THE BIBLE

Let us not love in word or talk but in deed and in truth.

—1 JOHN 3:18 ESV

* God, would you show me the ways you would like for me to share your love in practical ways? How can I use the opportunities, gifts, and talents you have given me on a daily basis to create spiritual conversations about you? Speak to me, Lord. I am listening.

* God, I pray you would show my husband the unique opportunities you give him every day to love others and point them to you.

TAKE ACTION

● Talk and pray with your husband about how the two of you might work together to combine your daily interests, passions, and lifestyle to cultivate friends who are not yet followers of Jesus. Make plans for building these friendships and sharing the love of Jesus.

CLAIM HIS PROMISES

I am not ashamed of the gospel, for it is the power of God for salvation to everyone who believes.

—ROMANS 1:16 ESV

Live His Mission M-1:
A Spirit-empowered disciple lives His mission by actively sharing their life with others and telling them about the Jesus who lives inside of them.

Day 29

EVERYDAY BLESSINGS

Actively share your life with others and tell them about the Jesus who lives in you.

STORIES FROM A WIFE'S HEART

Couples sometimes drift apart after several years of marriage. We've discovered a few ways that we can preserve the gift of love that God has given us. Preserving this gift requires that I remember my husband is my everyday blessing from God.

First, I need to verbalize my blessings. I let my spouse know that I miss him, I need him, I care about him, and I appreciate him. Gentle words are soothing, reassuring, and communicate that he's special to me. I also work hard to put my love into action. I regularly ask my husband how I can make our home more hospitable or comfortable for him. I ask him how I can better communicate my love in practical ways. I initiate conversations, listen attentively, and look for ways to say yes.

One critical thing that helps me remember the blessing of our marriage is to stay consistent in the small gestures of love. I welcome my husband when he comes home from work. I stop what I'm doing and greet him at the door. When I leave in the morning, I make sure to give him a kiss goodbye, and we end the day with an embrace and a prayer. I make eye contact when he's talking to me and make sure the kids know that dad and mom's conversations take priority. It's these small things that keep me grateful for the good gift that has been given to me—my husband!

PRAY: LISTEN TO JESUS

Look for people who might need you to share your life and the gospel. Begin by taking time to be with me. Next, be sure to share your life and the gospel with your husband, children, and family. Then you'll want to share the good news with neighbors, coworkers, and people of your community. Share not only the salvation story but also the everyday blessings I bring to your life. (See Matthew 28:19–20.)

* Jesus, make me more aware of the everyday blessings you bring to my life and give me opportunities to tell others about those blessings. I want to brag on you about _____.

* Lord, please make my husband more aware of the everyday blessings you bring to his life. Give him opportunities to tell others about those blessings. Empower him to _____.

LIVE: DO THE BIBLE

We loved you so much that we shared with you not only God's Good News but our own lives, too.

—1 THESSALONIANS 2:8

* God, show me who needs to hear your Good News and the ways you have blessed my life. Speak to me, Lord. I am listening. Give me opportunities and empowerment.

* Lord, please show my husband who needs to hear about your Good News and the ways you have blessed his life. Give him opportunities and empowerment.

TAKE ACTION

● First, talk with your husband about the ways that God has made a difference in your marriage, then look for opportunities to tell your Jesus story to another person or couple. Share how Jesus is changing you, your life, and your marriage.

● Look for ways to connect with unchurched couples. Invite them to your home, do life together, and share the hope that is within you.

CLAIM HIS PROMISES

Everything is from God, who reconciled us to himself through Christ and gave us the ministry of reconciliation.

—2 Corinthians 5:18 hcsb

Live His Mission M-1:

A Spirit-empowered disciple lives His mission by actively sharing their life with others and telling them about the Jesus who lives inside of them.

Day 30

MOVE TOWARD THE DIFFERENCES

Actively share your life with others and tell them about the Jesus who lives in you, especially as you celebrate how you and your husband are more alike than different.

STORIES FROM A WIFE'S HEART

When my husband was growing up, John Wayne was considered the archetypal American male. Strong, self-sufficient, and an independent thinker, he never admitted he needed anyone's help. My husband has given me approval to put this in print for the entire world to see: by John Wayne standards, he is not a real man. Why? Because he readily acknowledges that he wants and needs counsel from others, particularly from his wife. I thank God for the many times he has come to me with an issue or problem. He's needed and wanted my counsel because I see things from a different perspective.

In a similar way, he sees things in ways that I don't. I'm not as black and white as he is, and there are times when I need his perspective in order to make a decision or get clarity about next steps. I need his counsel on situations with my extended family because he has more objectivity and sees situations with less emotion. There have been hundreds of occasions when his wisdom has made the difference between good and bad decisions on my part.

We've learned that spouses need one another's counsel simply because each marriage partner has the advantage of differing perspectives on an issue. Listening to what my spouse tells me about a problem is often one of the wisest ways to go about solving it. So seek your spouse's counsel and offer yours. Move toward that differing perspective.

PRAY: LISTEN TO JESUS

You are my workmanship. Remember though, your husband is also my beautiful creation. Both of you were lovingly crafted with unique gifts, talents, and personalities. I've designed special purposes for each of you; I've created special plans for you to accomplish together. Come to me and listen. I'll share them with you. Celebrate the special plans I have ordained for you as a couple and then tell the world about the wonderful things we get to do together. (See Ephesians 2:10.)

* Jesus, remind me often of the special purposes you have designed for my husband. I celebrate the unique way he _____. We are certainly different in the way we _____, but what plans have you ordained for us together?

* Lord, reveal more of the special calling and purpose you have for my husband. Show him more of the plans you have ordained for us together.

LIVE: DO THE BIBLE

Tell of His glory among the nations,
His wonderful deeds among all the peoples.

—1 CHRONICLES 16:24 NASB

* God, as we come together in unity about the special plans you have for us, empower us to tell the world about your wonderful works. Give us opportunities to tell more people about the deeds you have done in our marriage.

* Lord, I pray you would bring unity and clarity of vision about how my husband and I share our faith with others. Let our unity be a confirmation of your plans and purposes.

TAKE ACTION

* Talk and pray with your husband about the celebrations of what the Lord has done in your marriage and how He has brought a beautiful story out of your differences.

* Pray together about how and where the Lord might want you to share your celebrations with others.

CLAIM HIS PROMISES

A spiritual gift is given to each of us so we can help each other.

—1 CORINTHIANS 12:7

Live His Mission M-1:
A Spirit-empowered disciple lives His mission by actively sharing their life with others and telling them about the Jesus who lives inside of them.

Day 31

KINDNESS
IS POWERFUL

Actively share your life with others and tell them about the Jesus who lives in you; specifically, share the gospel's power of kindness.

STORIES FROM A WIFE'S HEART

Jesus tells the story of a man who is robbed and left for dead on the side of the road. Two religious men walk past the injured man without offering help, but a man from Samaria shows kindness and offers aid. The Samaritan bandages his wounds, takes him to an inn, and provides for his continued care.

What did the Samaritan man have that the religious leaders lacked? What motivated him? I think it was that the Samaritan had encountered the miraculous love of God and that he had never gotten over the wonder of God's abundant care for him. He was grateful for what God had done for him, and that motivated him to care for others.

Are you still grateful for what God has done for you? Though you were still in sin, God selflessly gave His Son. Christ humbled Himself and left heaven to become a servant on your behalf because

His provision and care were exactly what you needed. He gave forgiveness, acceptance, love, and purpose in life.

Like the Samaritan, I can become genuinely sensitive to the needs of others—particularly my husband—by being mindful that I am a blessed recipient of God's abundant kindness.

It's sobering to think that because of Jesus, I hold within me the kindness my husband needs: acceptance, security, comfort, encouragement, care, and love. On the other hand, to withhold these blessings or to be insensitive to his needs is to behave just like the religious men of the Samaritan story who ignored the needs of the injured man and thought only of themselves.

PRAY: LISTEN TO JESUS

It will be my heart of love, expressed through my people, that will draw a searching world to ask about me. So first, remember my kindness. I have provided all the acceptance, support, and comfort you need. Spend time meditating on my kindness toward you, then demonstrate that kindness with your husband. It's great practice for sharing my kindness with others! When people who don't know me receive some of my acceptance, encouragement, comfort, and support delivered through you, they will begin to wonder where you got all that kindness. At that point, you'll be ready to talk about the hope that is inside you. It's their experience of kindness that opens the door for the gospel. (See 1 Peter 3:15; Romans 2:4, 15:7; Galatians 6:2; 2 Corinthians 1:3–4.)

* Jesus, I'm overwhelmed by your kindness toward me, specifically how you _____.

* Lord, reveal more of your kindness to my husband. Remind him of your _____.

LIVE: DO THE BIBLE

Do you think lightly of the riches of His kindness and tolerance and patience, not knowing that the kindness of God leads you to repentance?

—ROMANS 2:4 NASB

* God, because of your kindness toward me, I want to give more of your _____ to my husband. I also want to give more of your _____ to others, such as _____.

* Lord, overwhelm my husband with more of your kindness, as he gives more of your _____ to others.

TAKE ACTION

● Celebrate the powerful impact of kindness in your relationship. Talk and pray together about sharing your marriage story with others, giving testimony of the One who is the source of your joy.

CLAIM HIS PROMISES

You will be a witness for him to everyone of what you have seen and heard.

—ACTS 22:15 ESV

Live His Mission M-1:
A Spirit-empowered disciple lives His mission by actively sharing their life with others and telling them about the Jesus who lives inside of them.

ABOUT THE
GREAT COMMANDMENT NETWORK

The Great Commandment Network is an international collaborative network of strategic kingdom leaders from the faith community, marketplace, education, and caregiving fields who prioritize the powerful simplicity of the words of Jesus to love God, love others, and see others become His followers (Matthew 22:37–40, Matthew 28:19–20).

THE GREAT COMMANDMENT NETWORK IS SERVED THROUGH THE FOLLOWING:

Relationship Press – This team collaborates, supports, and joins together with churches, denominational partners, and professional associates to develop, print, and produce resources that facilitate ongoing Great Commandment ministry.

The Center for Relational Leadership – Their mission is to teach, train, and mentor both ministry and corporate leaders in Great Commandment principles, seeking to equip leaders with relational skills so they might lead as Jesus led.

The Galatians 6:6 Retreat Ministry – This ministry offers a unique two-day retreat for ministers and their spouses for personal renewal and for reestablishing and affirming ministry and family priorities.

The Center for Relational Care (CRC) – The CRC provides therapy and support to relationships in crisis through an accelerated process of growth and healing, including Relational Care Intensives for couples, families, and singles.

APPENDIX 2

A SPIRIT-EMPOWERED FAITH

Expresses Itself in Great Commission Living Empowered by Great Commandment Love

begins with the end in mind: The Great Commission calls us to make disciples.

"Go therefore and make disciples of all the nations, baptizing them in the name of the Father and the Son and the Holy Spirit teaching them to observe all things that I have commanded you; and lo, I am with you always, even to the end of the age." (Matthew 28:19–20)

The ultimate goal of our faith journey is to relate to the person of Jesus, because it is our relational connection to Jesus that will produce Christlikeness and spiritual growth. This relational perspective of discipleship is required if we hope to have a faith that is marked by the Spirit's power.

Models of discipleship that are based solely upon what we *know* and what we *do* are incomplete, lacking the empowerment of a life of loving and living intimately with Jesus. **A Spirit-empowered faith is relational and impossible to realize apart from a special work of the Spirit.** For example, the Spirit-empowered outcome of "listening to and hearing God" implies relationship—it is both relational in focus and requires the Holy Spirit's power to live.

begins at the right place: The Great Commandment calls us to start with loving God and loving others.

"'You shall love the Lord your God with all your heart, with all your soul, and with all your mind.' This is the first and great commandment. And the second is like it: 'You shall love your neighbor as yourself.' On these two commandments hang all the Law and the Prophets."
(Matthew 22:37–40)

Relevant discipleship does not begin with doctrines or teaching, parables or stewardship—but with loving the Lord with all your heart, mind, soul, and strength and then loving the people closest to you. Since Matthew 22:37–40 gives us the first and greatest commandment, *a Spirit-empowered faith starts where the Great Commandment tells us to start: A disciple must first learn to deeply love the Lord and to express His love to the "nearest ones"—his or her family, church, and community (and in that order).*

 embraces a relational process of Christlikeness.

Scripture reminds us that there are three sources of light for our journey: Jesus, His Word, and His people. The process of discipleship (or becoming more like Jesus) occurs as we relate intimately with each source of light.

"Walk while you have the light, lest darkness overtake you." (John 12:35)

Spirit-empowered discipleship will require a lifestyle of:
- Fresh encounters with Jesus (John 8:12)
- Frequent experiences of Scripture (Psalm 119:105)
- Faithful engagement with God's people (Matthew 5:14)

 can be defined with observable outcomes using a biblical framework.

The metrics for measuring Spirit-empowered faith or the growth of a disciple come from Scripture and are organized/framed around four distinct dimensions of a disciple who serves.

And He Himself gave some to be apostles, some prophets,
some evangelists, and some pastors and teachers,
for the equipping of the saints for the work of ministry,
for the edifying of the body of Christ.
(Ephesians 4:11–12)

A relational framework for organizing Spirit-Empowered Discipleship Outcomes draws from a cluster analysis of several Greek (*diakoneo, leitourgeo, douleuo*) and Hebrew words (*'abad, Sharat*), which elaborate on the Ephesians 4:12 declaration that Christ's followers are to be equipped for works of ministry or service. Therefore, the 40 Spirit-Empowered Faith Outcomes have been identified and organized around:

- Serving/loving the Lord – *While they were **ministering** to the Lord and fasting* (Acts 13:2 NASB).[1]
- Serving/loving the Word – *But we will devote ourselves to prayer and to the **ministry** of the word* (Acts 6:4 NASB).[2]
- Serving/loving people – *Through love **serve** one another* (Galatians 5:13 NASB).[3]
- Serving/loving His mission – *Now all these things are from God, who reconciled us to Himself through Christ and gave us the **ministry** of reconciliation* (2 Corinthians 5:18 NASB).[4]

---

1 Ferguson, David L. *Great Commandment Principle*. Cedar Park, Texas: Relationship Press, 2013.
2 Ferguson, David L. *Relational Foundations*. Cedar Park, Texas: Relationship Press, 2004.
3 Ferguson, David L. *Relational Discipleship*. Cedar Park, Texas: Relationship Press, 2005.
4 "Spirit Empowered Outcomes," www.empowered21.com, Empowered 21 Global Council, http://empowered21.com/discipleship-materials/.

A SPIRIT-EMPOWERED DISCIPLE LOVES THE LORD THROUGH

L1. Practicing thanksgiving in all things
Enter into His gates with thanksgiving (Ps. 100:4). *In everything give thanks* (1 Th. 5:18). *As sorrowful, yet always rejoicing* (2 Cor. 6:10).

L2. Listening to and hearing God for direction and discernment
"Speak, Lord, for Your servant hears" (1 Sam. 3:8–9). *Mary, who also sat at Jesus' feet and heard His word* (Lk. 10:38–42). *And the Lord said, "Shall I hide from Abraham what I am doing … ?"* (Gen. 18:17). *But as the same anointing teaches you concerning all things …* (1 Jn. 2:27).

L3. Experiencing God as He really is through deepened intimacy with Him
"Hear, O Israel: The Lord our God, the Lord is one! You shall love the Lord your God with all your heart, with all your soul, and with all your strength" (Deut. 6:4–5). *Therefore the Lord will wait, that He may be gracious to you; and therefore He will be exalted, that He may have mercy on you. For the Lord is a God of justice …* (Is. 30:18). See also John 14:9.

L4. Rejoicing regularly in my identity as "His Beloved"
And his banner over me was love (Song of Sol. 2:4). *To the praise of the glory of His grace, by which He made us accepted in the Beloved* (Eph. 1:6). *For so He gives His beloved sleep* (Ps. 127:2).

L5. Living with a passionate longing for purity and to please Him in all things
Who may ascend into the hill of the Lord? … He who has clean hands and a pure heart (Ps. 24:3–4). *Beloved, let us cleanse ourselves from all filthiness of flesh and spirit, perfecting holiness in the fear of God* (2 Cor. 7:1). *"I always do those things that please Him"* (Jn. 8:29). *"Though He slay me, yet will I trust Him"* (Job 13:15).

L6. Consistent practice of self-denial, fasting, and solitude rest

He turned and said to Peter, "Get behind me, Satan! You are offense to Me, for you are not mindful of the things of God, but the things of men" (Mt. 16:23). *"But you, when you fast …"* (Mt. 6:17). *"Be still, and know that I am God"* (Ps. 46:10).

L7. Entering often into Spirit-led praise and worship

Bless the LORD, O my soul, and all that is within me (Ps. 103:1). *Serve the LORD with fear* (Ps. 2:11). *I thank You, Father, Lord of heaven and earth* (Mt. 11:25).

L8. Disciplined, bold, and believing prayer

Praying always with all prayer and supplication in the Spirit (Eph. 6:18). *"Call to Me, and I will answer you"* (Jer. 33:3). *If we ask anything according to His will, He hears us. And if we know that He hears us, whatever we ask, we know that we have the petitions that we have asked of Him* (1 Jn. 5:14–15).

L9. Faithful stewardship and exercise of the gifts of the Spirit for empowered living and sacrifice

By one Spirit we were all baptized into one body—whether Jews or Greeks, whether slaves or free—and have all been made to drink into one Spirit (1 Cor. 12:13). *"But you shall receive power when the Holy Spirit has come upon you"* (Acts 1:8). *But the manifestation of the Spirit is given to each one for the profit of all* (1 Cor. 12:7). See also 1 Pet. 4:10 and Rom. 12:6.

L10. Practicing the presence of the Lord, yielding to the Spirit's work of Christlikeness

But we all, with unveiled face, … are being transformed into the same from glory to glory, just as by the Spirit of the Lord (2 Cor. 3:18). *As the deer pants for the water brooks, so pants my soul after You, O God* (Ps. 42:1).

A SPIRIT-EMPOWERED DISCIPLE
LIVES THE WORD THROUGH

W1. Frequently being led by the Spirit into deeper love for the One who wrote the Word

" 'You shall love the Lord your God … .' 'You shall love neighbor as yourself.' On these two commandments hang all the Law and the Prophets" (Mt. 22:37–40). *And I will delight myself in Your commandments, which I love.* (Ps. 119:47). *"The fear of the LORD is clean … . More to be desired are they than gold … sweeter also than honey"* (Ps. 19:9–10).

W2. Being a "living epistle" in reverence and awe as His Word becomes real in my life, vocation, and calling

You are our epistle written in our hearts, known and read by all men (2 Cor. 3:2). *And the Word became flesh and dwelt among us* (Jn. 1:14). *Husbands, love your wives … cleanse her with the washing of water by the word* (Eph. 5:25–26). *See also Tit. 2:5. And whatever you do, do it heartily, as to the Lord and not to men* (Col. 3:23).

W3. Yielding to the Scripture's protective cautions and transforming power to bring life change in me

Through Your precepts I get understanding; therefore I hate every false way (Ps. 119:104). *"Let it be to me according to your word"* (Lk. 1:38). *How can a young man cleanse his way? By taking heed according to Your word* (Ps. 119:9). See also Col. 3:16–17.

W4. Humbly and vulnerably sharing of the Spirit's transforming work through the Word

I will speak of your testimonies also before kings, and will not be ashamed (Ps. 119:46). *Preach the word! Be ready in season and out of season* (2 Tim. 4:2).

W5.   Meditating consistently on more and more of the Word hidden in the heart

Your word I have hidden in my heart, that I might not sin against You (Ps. 119:11). *Let the words of my mouth and the meditation of my heart be acceptable in Your sight, O Lord, my strength and my Redeemer* (Ps. 19:14).

W6.   Encountering Jesus in the Word for deepened transformation in Christlikeness

But we all, with unveiled face, … are being transformed into the same image from glory to glory, just as by the Spirit of the Lord (2 Cor. 3:18). *If you abide in Me, and My words abide in you, you will ask what you desire, and it shall be done for you* (Jn. 15:7). See also Lk. 24:32, Ps. 119:136, and 2 Cor. 1:20.

W7.   A life explained as one of "experiencing Scripture"

But this is what was spoken by the prophet Joel (Acts 2:16). *This is my comfort in my affliction, for Your word has given me life* (Ps. 119:50). *My soul breaks with longing for Your judgements at all times* (Ps. 119:20).

W8.   Living "naturally supernatural" in all of life as His Spirit makes the written Word (*logos*) the living Word (rhema)

So then aith comes by hearing, and hearing by the word (rhema) *of God* (Rom. 10:17). *Your word is a lamp to my feet and a light to my path* (Ps. 119:105).

W9.   Living abundantly "in the present" as His Word brings healing to hurt and anger, guilt, fear, and condemnation—which are heart hindrances to life abundant

"The thief does not come except to steal, and to kill, and to destroy" (Jn. 10:10). *I will run the course of Your commandments, for You shall enlarge my heart* (Ps. 119:32). *"And you shall know the truth, and the truth shall make you free"* (Jn. 8:32). *Stand fast therefore in the liberty by which Christ has made us free, and do not be entangled again with a yoke of bondage* (Gal. 5:1).

W10. Implicit, unwavering trust that His Word will never fail
"The grass withers, the flower fades, but the word of our God stands forever" (Is. 40:8). *"So shall My word be that goes forth from My mouth; it shall not return to Me void"* (Is. 55:11).

A SPIRIT-EMPOWERED DISCIPLE LOVES PEOPLE THROUGH

P1. Living a Spirit-led life of doing good in all of life: relationships and vocation, community and calling
Who went about doing good ... (Acts 10:38). *"Let your light so shine before men, that they may see your good works and glorify your Father in heaven"* (Mt. 5:16). *"But love your enemies, do good, and lend, hoping for nothing in return; and your reward will be great, and you will be sons of the Most High. For He is kind to the unthankful and evil"* (Lk. 6:35). See also Rom. 15:2.

P2. "Startling people" with loving initiatives to "give first"
"Give, and it will be given to you: good measure, pressed down, shaken together, and running over will be put into your bosom" (Lk. 6:38). *Then Jesus said, "Father, forgive them, for they do not know what they do"* (Lk. 23:34). See also Lk. 23:43 and Jn. 19:27.

P3. Discerning the relational needs of others with a heart to give of His love
Let no corrupt word proceed out of your mouth, but what is good for necessary edification, that it might impart grace to the hearers (Eph. 4:29). *And my God shall supply all your need according to His riches in glory by Christ Jesus* (Phil. 4:19). See also Lk. 6:30.

P4.   Seeing people as needing BOTH redemption from sin AND intimacy in relationships, addressing both human fallen-ness and aloneness
But God demonstrates His own love toward us, in that while we were still sinners, Christ died for us (Rom. 5:8). *And when Jesus came to the place, He looked up and saw him, and said to him, "Zacchaeus, make haste and come down, for today I must stay at your house"* (Lk. 19:5). See also Mk. 8:24 and Gen. 2:18.

P5.   Ministering His life and love to our nearest ones at home and with family as well as faithful engagement in His body, the church
Husbands, likewise, dwell with them with understanding, giving honor to the wife, as to the weaker vessel, and as being heirs together of the grace of life, that your prayers may not be hindered (1 Pet. 3:7). See also 1 Pet. 3:1 and Ps. 127:3.

P6.   Expressing the fruit of the Spirit as a lifestyle and identity
But the fruit of the Spirit is love, joy, peace, longsuffering, kindness, goodness, faithfulness, gentleness, self-control (Gal. 5:22–23). *A man's stomach shall be satisfied from the fruit of his mouth; From the produce of his lips he shall be filled* (Prov. 18:20).

P7.   Expecting and demonstrating the supernatural as His spiritual gifts are made manifest and His grace is at work by His Spirit
In mighty signs and wonders, by the power of the Spirit of God, so that from Jerusalem and round about to Illyricum I have fully preached the gospel of Christ (Rom. 15:19). *"Most assuredly, I say to you, he who believes in Me, the works that I do he will do also"* (Jn. 14:12). See also 1 Cor. 14:1.

P8.   Taking courageous initiative as a peacemaker, reconciling relationships along life's journey
Be at peace among yourselves (1 Th. 5:13). *For He Himself is our peace, who has made both one, and has broken down the middle wall of separation* (Eph. 2:14). *Confess your trespasses to one another, and pray for one another, that you may be healed* (Jas. 5:16).

P9. Demonstrating His love to an ever growing network of "others" as He continues to challenge us to love "beyond our comfort"

He who says, "I know Him," and does not keep His commandments, is a liar, and the truth is not in him (1 Jn. 2:4). If someone says, "I love God," and hates his brother, he is a liar; for he who does not love his brother whom he has seen, how can he love God whom he has not seen? (1 Jn. 4:20).

P10. Humbly acknowledging to the Lord, ourselves, and others that it is Jesus in and through us who is loving others at their point of need

"Take My yoke upon you and learn from Me, for I am gentle and lowly in heart, and you will find rest for your souls" (Mt. 11:29). "If I then, your Lord and Teacher, have washed your feet, you also ought to wash one another's feet" (Jn. 13:14).

A SPIRIT-EMPOWERED DISCIPLE LIVES HIS MISSION THROUGH

M1. Imparting the gospel and one's very life in daily activities and relationships, vocation and community

So, affectionately longing for you, we were well pleased to impart to you not only the gospel of God, but also our own lives, because you had become dear to us (1 Th. 2:8–9). See also Eph. 6:19.

M2. Expressing and extending the kingdom of God as compassion, justice, love, and forgiveness are shared

"I must preach the kingdom of God to the other cities also, because for this purpose I have been sent" (Lk. 4:43). "As You sent Me into the world, I also have sent them into the world" (Jn. 17:18). Restore to me the joy of Your salvation, and uphold me by Your generous Spirit. Then I will teach transgressors Your ways, and sinners shall be converted to You (Ps. 51:12–13). See also Mic. 6:8.

M3. Championing Jesus as the only hope of eternal life and abundant living

"Nor is there salvation in any other, for there is no other name under heaven given among men by which we must be saved" (Acts 4:12). *"The thief does not come except to steal, and to kill, and to destroy. I have come so that they may have life, and that they have it more abundantly"* (Jn. 10:10). See also Acts 4:12 and Jn. 14:6.

M4. Yielding to the Spirit's role to convict others as He chooses, resisting expressions of condemnation

"And when He has come, He will convict the world of sin, and of righteousness, and of judgment" (Jn. 16:8). *Who is he who condemns? It is Christ who died, and furthermore is also risen, who is even at the right hand of God, who also makes intercession for us* (Rom. 8:34). See also Rom. 8:1.

M5. Ministering His life and love to the "least of these"

"Then He will answer them saying, 'Assuredly, I say to you inasmuch as you did not do it to one of the least of these, you did not do it to Me'" (Mt. 25:45). *Pure and undefiled religion before God and the Father is this: to visit orphans and widows in their trouble, and to keep oneself unspotted from the world* (Jas. 1:27).

M6. Bearing witness of a confident peace and expectant hope in God's lordship in all things

Now may the Lord of peace Himself give you peace always in every way. The Lord be with you all (2 Thess. 3:16). *And let the peace of God rule in your hearts, to which also you were called in one body; and be thankful* (Col. 3:15). See also Rom. 8:28 and Ps. 146:5.

M7. Faithfully sharing of time, talent, gifts, and resources in furthering His mission

Of which I became a minister according to the stewardship from God which was given to me for you, to fulfill the word of God (Col. 1:25). *"For everyone to whom much is given, from him much will be required"* (Lk. 12:48). See also 1 Cor. 4:1–2.

M8.   Attentive listening to others' story, vulnerably sharing of our story, and a sensitive witness of Jesus' story as life's ultimate hope; developing your story of prodigal, preoccupied and pain-filled living; listening for others' story and sharing Jesus' story

But sanctify the Lord God in your hearts, and always be ready to give a defense to everyone who asks you a reason for the hope that is in you, with meekness and fear (1 Pet. 3:15). *"For this my son was dead and is alive again"* (Luke 15:24). See also Mk. 5:21–42 and Jn. 9:1–35.

M9.   Pouring our life into others, making disciples who in turn make disciples of others

"Go therefore and make disciples of all the nations, baptizing them in the name of the Father and of the Son and of the Holy Spirit, teaching them to observe all things that I commanded you; and lo, I am with you always, even to the end of the age" (Mt. 28:19–20). See also 2 Tim. 2:2.

M10. Living submissively within His body, the Church, as instruction and encouragement; reproof and correction are graciously received by faithful disciples

Submitting to one another in the fear of God (Eph. 5:21). *Brethren, if a man is overtaken in any trespass, you who are spiritual restore such a one in a spirit of gentleness, considering yourself lest you also be tempted* (Gal. 6:1). See also Gal. 6:2.

Notes

Notes

Notes

Notes

Notes

Notes

Notes